HEATH ROBINSON'S COMMERCIAL ART

A COMPENDIUM OF HIS ADVERTISING WORK

HEATH ROBINSON'S COMMERCIAL ART

A COMPENDIUM OF HIS ADVERTISING WORK

GEOFFREY BEARE

LUND HUMPHRIES

FOR EMMA

First published in 2017 by Lund Humphries
Lund Humphries
Office 3, Book House
261A City Road
London
EC1V 1JX
UK

www.lundhumphries.com

© Geoffrey Beare, 2017
Foreword © Peter Lord

ISBN: 978-1-84822-216-8
A Cataloguing-in-Publication record for this
book is available from the British Library

Copy edited by Abigail Grater
Designed by Nigel Soper
Set in Utopia, Gill Sans Nova and Paddington
Printed in Slovenia

Front Cover:
'An Antiquated Method of Filling
the Boilers without Stopping the
Engine Before the Introduction of
the Water Trough System', from
Railway Ribaldry, 1935.

Inside front cover flap:
Heath Robinson photographed
by Bertram Park, 1915.

Back Cover:
From the cover of the booklet
*Behind The Scenes at Moss Bros
with Heath Robinson*, 1936.

Frontispiece:
Heath Robinson at work in his
studio, 1929.

CONTENTS

FOREWORD

Peter Lord, who with Dave Sproxton and Nick Park worked as producer,
editor and director on the *Wallace and Gromit* and *Chicken Run* films, talks
about Heath Robinson's influence on their work.

Dave Sproxton and I, the two partners at
Ardman, became interested in Heath
Robinson's work in the late 1960s, when we
were at school together. Penguin published a book
of his work, *the Penguin Heath Robinson*, in 1966,
which I still own to this day. It was loved by kids of
our age and incredibly influential on our later work
and certainly on the work of Nick Park, who joined
Ardman in 1985, bringing with him Wallace and
Gromit, his creations, and their love of contraptions.

I cannot really overstate the impact upon me of
that first exposure to Heath Robinson's works at the
age of 12. At that age, the mind is impressionable and
the world's cultures and possibilities are opening
up to you, whether that be in art, popular music
or cinema. In the realm of comedy, entranced by
his graphic flair and skill as a story teller, Heath
Robinson became my idol.

I say story teller advisedly, because you really
do have to read his drawings and realise there is a
narrative in there. They are jokes to be read in time
and space, the eye tracking around from one detail
to another, where immensely complex machines
work the entirety of their physical splendour to
achieve something rather small, and maybe even
quite banal. It is the set-up of these visual jokes, and
the surprising turns they take, that I find profoundly
funny, whilst marvelling at the sheer imagination
behind their creation.

The same principles can be found in Ardman-
produced films. There are different levels of detail to
be read by the viewer: a surface narrative and focus
of action in the foreground, certainly, but then there
is often so much additional, delightful surrounding
detail for people to enjoy. To take an example, in
the film *Chicken Run*, the titular birds make their
escape from captivity on the Tweedy's farm in a
hand-made – or should I say 'wing-made' – plane.
On the surface, an action set piece full of tension. But
look more closely and you see these rather skilful
chickens have made their vehicle from scrap. They
have demolished their chicken huts, and found old
rubbish lying around the farmyard from which they
have fashioned cogs and gears turned by drive belts
of ropes with knots in them. Pure Heath Robinson!

Another key resonance of Heath Robinson's work
for us at Ardman is the uniquely British character,
both of his inventions and their settings and the
figures that operate and embody them. He had a
wonderful eye for the unique and everyday details
of his particular era; of the expressions, ticks and
quirks of flat-capped factory workers straining to
pull levers, of bespectacled distillers huddled over
bubbling vats or the rather formal, rather boring
looking middle-classes playing bridge or taking their
afternoon tea.

Tucking and squeezing these figures around the
edges or in the interstices between the components
of his sprawling machines, pits their deadpan,
but rather charming British propriety against the
crackpot inventiveness of British industry. Two
received notions of the national character are pitted
against each other, to great comic effect, in a very
smart, yet very affectionate comment on Britishness.
This sense of humour I think is similar to Ardman's.
There are many different aspects to British humour,
some of it quite dark and sarcastic, but Heath
Robinson's is gentle and charming. I don't see much
of a hard edge in there, which is partly why we love
to come back to his work. I do feel absolutely part of

Heath Robinson's "Ideal Home." THE DINING ROOM.

Daily Mail Ideal Home Exhibition, OLYMPIA, W., 1934.

the same tradition as him – completely, profoundly – and also in his debt. So much of what we do is very much derived from him. I am proud to feel part of the same artistic tradition as Heath Robinson. As the father of an entire notion of eccentric machinery and with a huge body of work, of which each individual piece seems a universe in itself, unquestionably his work will inspire new generations as it once captivated and continues to fascinate me.

PETER LORD, interviewed for the Heath Robinson Museum

2 'Kippering Herrings by the Side of the River Yare', an early example of Heath Robinson's contraption pictures, published in *The Sketch*, December 1908.

INTRODUCTION

This is the first book to provide a complete overview of Heath Robinson's commercial art and includes a detailed listing of his published drawings for advertising. Based on over 30 years of collecting and research, it offers an appreciation of the true significance of his advertising work both in terms of his career and the influence it had on the way advertising functioned during his lifetime and beyond. It includes a large number of Heath Robinson images that have never been reproduced since their first appearance in obscure trade publications, including many of his finest contraption drawings. It is also the first book to have colour reproductions of some of Heath Robinson's finest works.

Heath Robinson's name has entered the language to describe any contraption made from whatever materials come to hand, usually held together with knotted string. But who was he? William Heath Robinson (1872–1944) was a brilliant artist whose initial ambition was to be a landscape painter. However, having no private income, he had to earn a living. He worked first as an illustrator and by the early 1900s was ranked with Arthur Rackham (1867–1939) and Edmund Dulac (1882–1953) as one of the leading illustrators of the age. The failure of a publisher to pay him for a major project led him to try his hand at humorous art, and in a short time he was being fêted as a unique talent in this field too. His subjects were human nature and particularly those individuals who had an inflated view of their own importance. He quickly discovered that this could be demonstrated through over-complicated machinery, and so were born the Heath Robinson gadgets and contraptions for which he was to become famous. They first appeared in the pages of *The Sketch* magazine in 1906 in a series of drawings titled 'The Gentle Art of Catching Things'. As early as 1908 a commentator in the *London Magazine* observed that: 'He has opened a rich vein of humour in which he disports himself diligently – and alone. His power of comic invention and his method of expression are alike unique'.[1]

From 1905 to 1920 he was able to pursue parallel careers as both serious illustrator and humorous artist. Thereafter he was mostly reliant on his work as a humorist to earn a living, although he grasped any opportunity for serious illustration that presented itself and he continued to paint both landscapes and imagined scenes throughout his life.

At the time of his death in 1944 he was known as 'The Gadget King' and, although he did not know it, the first electronic code-breaking computer at Bletchley Park had just been named after him. At the Ideal Home Exhibition in 1934 one of the show houses had been Heath Robinson's Ideal Home, 'The Gadgets'. Based on his drawings and built by a firm of engineers, it had more than 30 lifelike moving figures operating various contraptions. In particular, Mother and Father dropped through the bedroom floor to the dining room below for breakfast, lifting the covers from their food, turning on the radio and feeding the cat as they went. This was clearly the inspiration for the opening scenes of the Wallace and Gromit film *The Wrong Trousers* (1993).

Heath Robinson's work, both in illustration and humour, was popular in the US in the first part of the 20th century, with most of his illustrated books being co-published by American publishers and his cartoons being syndicated in *Life* and other US magazines. He was also commissioned by periodicals such as *Harper's Bazaar* to illustrate articles in his comic style. However, from about 1928 he was supplanted by a cartoonist called Ruben Garrett Lucius ('Rube') Goldberg (1883–1970) as 'gadget master' in the US press. Goldberg, who graduated as an engineer and first worked in San Francisco for the Water and Sewers Department, switched career to become a sports cartoonist. In 1928 he invented a character called Professor Lucifer G. Butts who made screwball machines, and in 1931 Goldberg's name entered the dictionary to describe the accomplishment of something simple through complex means. Heath Robinson and Goldberg are often compared, but at heart they are very different. Goldberg was an engineer who drew cartoons, while Heath Robinson was an artist who drew some contraptions. Goldberg's gadget drawings are always accompanied by detailed explanations of how they work, and the drawing style is that of the 1930s comic strip. Heath Robinson's inventions are beautifully rendered, often set in finely depicted landscapes or townscapes and need no explanation. The humour depends on the fact that there is no hint of the comic in the way they are drawn.

One consequence of Heath Robinson's diversion into humorous art was that he was drawn into the world of advertising. During the early years of the 20th century companies gradually started to use humorous artists to advertise their products and, from about 1920, the use of humour in advertising was generally accepted. For the artists this work would have been an important source of income, especially as work used for advertising was generally better paid than equivalent magazine contributions. Heath Robinson was first introduced to advertising in 1903, when the modern approach to the subject was in its infancy, and he worked for a wide range of companies until shortly before his death in 1944. As he said in his autobiography: 'Steel girders, Swiss rolls, welding, toffee, papermaking, marmalade, asbestos cement, beef essence, motor spirit and lager beer were among the many and diverse subjects to be treated.'[2]

Much of this work was published in trade journals or in booklets to be distributed at trade exhibitions, which meant that it had a limited circulation. Where his work did reach a wider public it was in newspapers or in the advertising pages of popular magazines which, even if the editorial matter was preserved in volume form, would often have been discarded prior to binding. If companies kept publicity archives or took care of the original artwork, such resources have rarely survived the takeovers, mergers and economy drives of recent years. It therefore requires a major effort over many years to build a comprehensive collection of the advertising work of a humorous artist. Nevertheless, to do so can be very rewarding. The high fees paid and the relatively high quality of the reproduction methods used mean that such a collection will contain much of the artist's best and most imaginative work. This is certainly the case for Heath Robinson.

FIRST STEPS

William Heath Robinson was born into a family of artists in Finsbury Park, North London, on 31 May 1872. His father, Thomas, worked for the *Penny Illustrated Paper*, providing the illustration for its leading news story each week. His uncle Charles worked as a book illustrator and was a regular contributor to the *Illustrated London News*. On leaving school at the age of 15, William started his training as an artist at the Islington School of Art and spent time drawing in the British Museum. This prepared him for admission to the Royal Academy Schools, which he achieved at his second attempt. He received rigorous training as a draughtsman, and particularly enjoyed the classes in life drawing and painting. On leaving art school in 1897, his ambition was to become a landscape painter, but he soon realised that such work would not pay the bills. He therefore decided to join his two older brothers, Tom and Charles, and become an illustrator.

Heath Robinson was fortunate in leaving art school at a time when two revolutions in illustration were taking place. There was a technical revolution as photomechanical or process engraving displaced the wood engraving that had been the main method of reproducing drawings for the past 50 years. With it went an older generation of artists who had relied on the wood engraver to finish their drawings for them. In parallel was a stylistic revolution in which the dull realist manner of illustrating books and magazines that had prevailed through the 1870s and 1880s was swept aside in favour of a more romantic and decorative style. Heath Robinson quickly proved himself adept at mastering the requirements of process engraving and at exploiting the possibilities of the new art movement. These qualities, combined with his rigorous training in classical composition and drawing, his family grounding in the disciplines of commercial art and most importantly his fertile imagination and unique sense of humour, ensured that he rapidly prospered in the commercial market.

It was a burgeoning market, particularly for young artists who could adapt the style of their drawings to the demands of the new photographic methods of reproduction, and Heath Robinson was not slow to find work. His first published drawings, made while still at art school, had illustrated a serial story in the *Sunday Magazine* in 1896. He quickly established himself as one of the leading illustrators of the day, and when his illustrated edition of *The Poems of Edgar Allen Poe* was published in 1900, *The Studio* magazine described him as a 'worthy disciple of the modern school of penmen'.[3]

In 1902 Heath Robinson approached the publisher Grant Richards with a children's book that he had both written and illustrated called *The Adventures of Uncle Lubin*. Richards was enthusiastic about the book, and by September it was in print, ready for the Christmas market (fig.3). It tells the story of an old man whose nephew, baby Peter, is stolen by the wicked Bag-bird and of his search for the child and his eventual recovery. It was a remarkable production, designed from cover to cover by the artist and visually stunning throughout. Following the success of Uncle Lubin, Heath Robinson illustrated two more children's books for Grant Richards and then, in 1903, was set to work to illustrate a large and finely printed edition of *The Works of Rabelais* with 100 full-page drawings and over 150 headpieces and vignettes (fig.6). Writing to the US publisher J.P. Lippincott seeking a co-publication deal, Richards said that: 'my own interest in the production is limited to my admiration for Mr. Heath Robinson's work and my anxiety to give him this chance of producing what I think will be a really fine monument, for I never could read Rabelais and I don't suppose I ever shall be able to.'[4] Sadly, no deal was forthcoming and the cost of publishing the book contributed to the failure of the firm of Grant Richards. Heath Robinson had received a small advance, but was left without payment for a substantial body of work. He was recently married with a young child, and turned to the upmarket weekly magazines that were always in need of humorous drawings and paid in cash on delivery. He thus launched a second career, that of humorous artist, which he conducted in parallel with his activities as an illustrator. In his autobiography

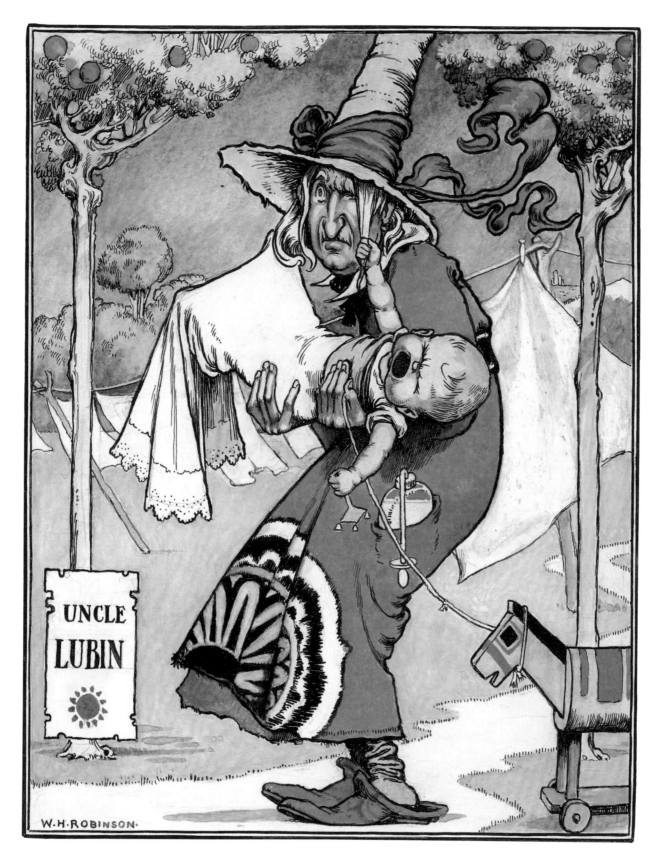

3 The frontispiece for
*The Adventures of Uncle
Lubin*, 1902, pen and
watercolour,
190 × 235 mm
(7½ × 9¼ in).

he writes: 'One day I might be illustrating Kipling's *A Song of the English* or a Shakespeare play and the next would find me at work explaining the Gentle Art of Catching something. It was always a mental effort to adapt myself to these changes, but with the elasticity of my early days, it was not too difficult.'[5]

The publication of *The Adventures of Uncle Lubin* led to a highly beneficial commission. In 1903 a letter arrived from someone called Chas. Ed. Potter who, on reading the book, had decided that Heath Robinson was the artist to illustrate some advertisements he was writing. Potter was an American, and having heard tales of wily American confidence tricksters, Robinson was suspicious. He agreed to make the drawings on condition that he received cash payment for each one as it was delivered. Cash in those days meant solid gold, and in his autobiography he recalls that:

Chas. Ed. Potter appeared to see nothing unusual in these stipulations and readily agreed to them, though I fancy a twinkle of amusement escaped through the gold-rimmed glasses. Every two or three days for the next few weeks I called at the hotel with my drawings. One of us seated on a chair and the other on the bed, we then discussed and planned the next set.[6]

Potter was working for the Lamson Paragon Supply Company of Canning Town, London. The company manufactured 'Check Books', which enabled traders to keep detailed records of their transactions, 'Plic Books' which would give a carbon duplicate from a pen-and-ink written original, and paper bags. The first example of their collaboration was published in the *Drapers' Record* on 25 April 1903 (fig.4). A man is about to snip off a shopkeeper's ear, and the text underneath promoting Paragon Check Books began: 'Are you satisfied with your sales system? If you are, don't waste time reading further. We want the ear of the progressive shopkeeper – the one who is not satisfied.' Drawings in a similar vein encouraging traders to use Paragon Check Books appeared for the next seven weeks, and the series was then reused. Potter left London in April 1903. His successor was a New Yorker called John Meath Evans. Soon after taking up his new post with Lamson Paragon, Evans contacted Heath Robinson who invited him to work in his studio. Evans would visit Heath Robinson weekly to collect drawings and plan the next set (figs 274, 276–82). Following his company's business principles, he used a 'Plic' book to record their discussions, giving Heath Robinson one copy and keeping the other. Subjects were sometimes quotations from the classics, but were frequently fresh ideas. Themes that were often used

4 Heath Robinson's first drawing for the Lamson Paragon Company, 1903.

5 A drawing and inscription from the copy of his autobiography that Heath Robinson sent to John Meath Evans in 1941. The inscription reads 'In memory of our friendly collaboration of many years ago'.

To J. M. Evans.
In memory of our friendly collaboration of many years ago
W.H.R.
1941.

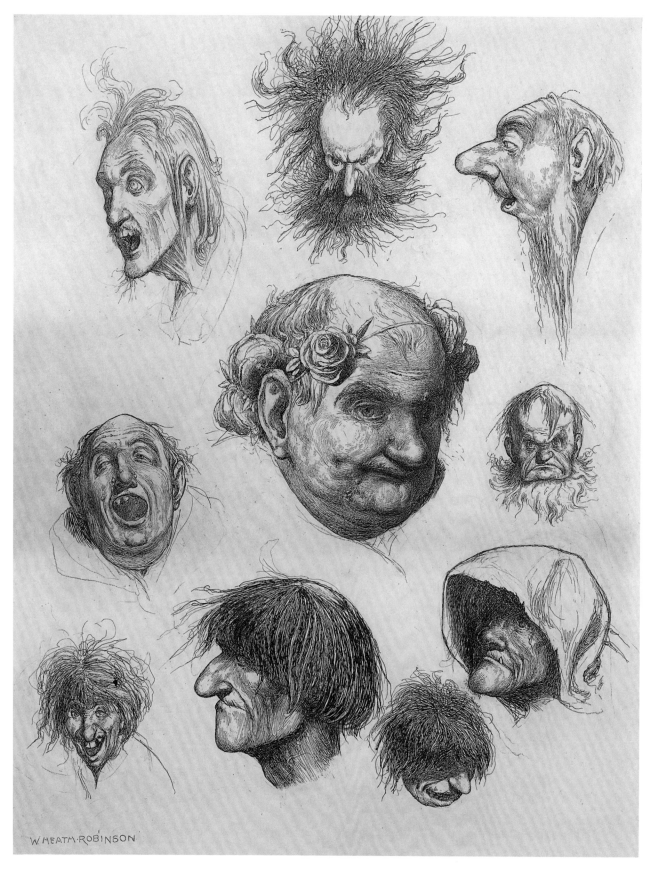

6 Studies of grotesque
heads for *Rabelais*, 1904,
pen and ink,
425 × 520 mm
(16¾ × 20½ in).

W.HEATH·ROBINSON

included lack of profits because the shopkeeper did not have the security that a check book system would provide; the inefficiency of making manual copies or using a copying press – a 'Plic' book would be quicker; and dangers of economising by using inferior materials such as cheap paper bags that spill customers' goods, thereby risking their goodwill to save a few pence.

AN ESTABLISHED TALENT

He continued to produce work for Lamson Paragon alongside his other projects until 1907, when much of his time was taken up with a commission from Hodder and Stoughton to make 40 coloured illustrations for *Twelfth Night*. This was the first of a series of *de luxe* illustrated gift books with texts by Shakespeare, Kipling, Andersen and the artist himself. These commissions continued until 1914, when the onset of war all but killed the market for such luxuries. Heath Robinson was too old to take an active part in the conflict, but through his pen he made a contribution to maintaining the morale of both servicemen and civilians that far outweighed anything he could have done in uniform.

In December 1915 a journalist called Lampeter Todd wrote an article in the *Advertising World* magazine recommending advertisers to employ Heath Robinson, claiming that:

> no man's work has more power to attract the vagrant eye and rivet the wandering attention of all sorts and conditions of gentle readers.
>
> The outstanding characteristic of his humorous work is its entire gravity, the 'really and truly' atmosphere with which he invests the most fantastic creations of his imagination. He loves to express a whimsical idea, always

perfectly simple in itself, by exhibiting it with a host of its implications; and to support his main theme by a wealth of the natural variations that arise from it.

> He should be induced to do more for the advertiser; more especially, perhaps, as a humorous draughtsman, for there he brings to the service of those who use his work the value of a reputation that is practically world-wide, in addition to the intrinsic worth of his productions.[7]

Todd also expressed the wish to see Heath Robinson posters on the hoardings, and stated that these should not be in his humorous style, but should capitalise on his 'fine sense of structural design, his exceptional skill in handling broad, flat masses, and the simple directness with which he expresses himself in line and tone', which all indicated that he could be 'a designer of posters of distinction far beyond the ordinary'. However, apart from a few theatrical posters between 1904 and 1913, Heath Robinson was not tempted to undertake poster work.

Heath Robinson's success as an advertising artist was due to his skills as a draughtsman combined with his imagination and gentle sense of humour. However, as Christopher Mann observed in *Commercial Art* magazine in June 1927, it was also the way his work could engage the casual observer that was essential to that success. He writes:

> Mr. Heath Robinson's drawings have one great advantage as a form of advertisement, they cannot be skipped. There are any number of faultless works of art illustrating the virtues of commercial products over which the eye merely skims, passing on to something else. But

a Heath Robinson must be examined minutely. There is something indescribably fascinating in the apparatus which his pen invents. One must follow that mysterious thread from its source, see (breathlessly) how it passes over pulleys and round cylinders, note with anxiety the ominous knots which hold its length together, observe it rotating round a final spool and perform at length the operation of working a soda-water syphon. No detail has been overlooked. Every practical contingency is provided for. A great mechanical inventor, it is evident, was lost to the world in this artist. But if he cannot make actual machines he can draw marvellous plans of imaginary ones, which simply insist on examination and approval. His fictions have more reality than fact. There is a mad but convincing logic even in his wildest flights. Each part of a fantastic scaffolding dovetails with the other parts, and the most improbable operation of his engines is circumstantial.[8]

Of course this is not only the case with his contraptions. It equally applies to his other drawings in which there is a wealth of detail to be discovered. Mann goes on to say:

> Humour, of course, is a somewhat dangerous vehicle for conveying the merits of serious matters like printing ink, warehouses, soap and motor-cars. It would never do for the public to think that your wonderful new car was a joke, or to cause a roar of laughter amongst printers at the name of your special new ink. How it is we cannot exactly say (and yet it is so) the Heath Robinson advertisement seems to act by opposites. Its absurdities are convincing, and yet one is the reverse of convinced that what is advertised is an absurdity. One retains the idea that the ink or the car has been well and carefully prepared with all that human ingenuity can do, without an uneasy suspicion that the engine is screwed on to the car in some totally ridiculous manner by an aged person in a top hat, or that fat men in the employ of Messrs. Shuck Maclean pound ink by the primitive procedure of stamping on it with their feet.

THE TWELVE VIRTUES OF CHAIRMAN.
No. 12.—It is an economy.

Chairman goes twice as far as an ordinary tobacco. This is due to its perfect combustion. It burns slowly and evenly to the last shred. The pipe is the most economical form of smoking—Chairman is the most economical of pipe tobaccos. Each ounce yields a full six hours of enjoyment and costs but eightpence.

And it has other fine qualities—it pleases the palate with its flavour and its clean and fragrant aroma is a delight which others than the smoker may enjoy.

The pleasures it gives are constant with every pipe, no matter how much it may be smoked, as it is always cool to the tongue.

It is made in different strengths to meet the tastes of most men—"Chairman," medium; "Boardman's," mild; and "Recorder," full—and is sold at 8d. per oz. in 1 and 2 oz. lead packets, and at 2/7 per ¼-lb. in ¼, ½ and 1-lb. canisters by all principal tobacconists and stores.

Also sold by principal dealers in Canada, Australia, New Zealand, India, Egypt, S. Africa, France, Norway, Sweden and the Far East.

R. J. LEA, LIMITED, MANCHESTER.

7 One of the series of drawings promoting the virtues of 'Chairman' tobacco that appeared in *Punch* and other magazines in 1915–16.

8 'The Making of Johnnie Walker Whisky: In the filtering vaults at Kilmarnock', 1915.

that showed the virtues of tobacco and stages in the whisky-making process. The set of 12 drawings that he made to advertise Chairman tobacco are wonderfully imaginative in the number of ways that they display its unique qualities, sustaining the surreal element that was present in much of his early humorous work (figs 7 and 247–55). However, it was the six drawings that he made to promote Johnnie Walker whisky that really set the scene for much of his future advertising work, employing his mechanical inventiveness to show the making of the whisky as it might be in a Heath Robinson world (figs 8 and 72–7).

In 1921 he was commissioned by the toffee makers John Mackintosh & Sons to make a drawing of his idea of how Mackintosh's Toffee de Luxe is made. Heath Robinson called his drawing *A Half Hour in Toffee Town*, and with a series of six small line drawings in a single frame showed the stages in the toffee-making process. The final vignette was testing, in which the power of the toffees to placate crying infants was assessed (see fig.64). The drawing filled the front page of the *Daily Mail* and other papers, as well as appearing in various upmarket magazines, and the format was frequently repeated for various customers.

Heath Robinson's humorous drawings were much in demand for magazines during the First World War, and the positive effect that they had on raising morale is evidenced by the many letters that he received, both thanking him for bringing a little brightness in such difficult times, and also offering suggestions for future drawings. This impact was recognised by companies keen to capture some of his magic, and his career as an advertising artist really took off with commissions to make drawings

In the years following the First World War the demand for illustrated books diminished and Heath Robinson depended to a greater extent on his humorous work. While commissions from magazines such as *The Bystander*, *The Strand*, *Pearson's* and *The Humorist* occupied much of his time, it was the commercial work that paid the best and which inspired his most inventive ideas. An unusual commission came in 1930 when he was asked by the Canadian Pacific Railway Company to decorate the cocktail bar and the children's room on their latest transatlantic liner, the *Empress of*

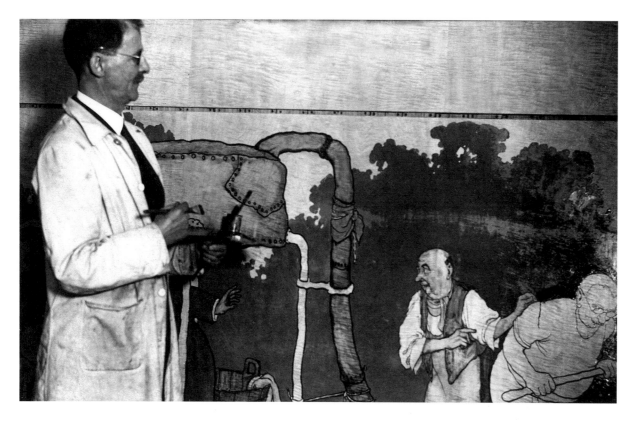

9 Heath Robinson at work on one of the panels for the cocktail bar on the *Empress of Britain*, 1930.

Britain. He was particularly inspired by the cocktail bar (figs 9 and 182–7). Around the walls were a series of pictures showing, in typical Heath Robinson style, how cocktails are made. However, on looking up, drinkers would see a number of openings which were decorated with *trompe-l'oeil* paintings of the sky with a parachutist dropping in, ramshackle aircraft passing over or loungers sitting dangling their feet and looking down. Very disconcerting, especially after the third Martini!

Another commercial commission at about the same time as the *Empress of Britain* project was to design a range of nursery china decorated with nursery rhymes and a frieze of children's faces. There were 16 different nursery rhymes illustrated on a wide variety of pieces. Initially the china, which was manufactured by the Crown Ducal factory in Stoke-on-Trent, was exclusive to the Soane & Smith department store in Knightsbridge, London, but later the nursery designs were reused on items that were less well made and without the frieze of faces. This was sold through a range of outlets.

In 1935 the Great Western Railway celebrated its centenary and commissioned Heath Robinson to make a book of drawings (see figs 188–94). Titled *Railway Ribaldry*, it showed the history of the company, its current operations and ways in which it might expand in the future.

Heath Robinson continued to be in demand for advertising work throughout the inter-war years and his last commission in 1941 was to make a series of drawings for a company called High Duty Alloys that manufactured components for aircraft (figs 10 and 202–9). The series of eight drawings titled 'The War in the Air' took phrases of RAF jargon or slang and illustrated each with an appropriate drawing in his inimitable style. They were published in *Flight* and *Aeroplane* magazines.

For Heath Robinson his commercial work was of great benefit, but not without its drawbacks. It was a blessing in providing him with a substantial income at a time when the market for his style of illustration had dwindled. It also allowed him to present his humorous work to the public in much

'THE WAR IN THE AIR' BY W·HEATH·ROBINSON

Nº 3
TO BALE OUT
IS TO LEAVE THE
PLANE AT A MOMENT'S
NOTICE WHEN YOUR
SERVICES ARE
REQUIRED ELSEWHERE

10 An advertisement for High Duty Alloys aircraft component manufacturer, 1941.

clear from surviving correspondence that he found it tedious working for companies with a top-heavy management structure whose managers or directors all had to put in their two penn'orth of comment on his designs, leading to repeated requests for changes. It must sometimes have been tedious to be asked to devise the umpteenth set of wheels and pulleys to represent the making of macaroni or the bleaching of cloth. However, he took pride in delivering the best possible product and delighted in adding humorous details in the backgrounds of the drawings.

William Heath Robinson is an artist of international standing and his work, whether in his well-known humorous drawings or his illustrations for Kipling, Shakespeare or his own children's stories, is integral to the fabric of British cultural heritage. His name entered the language as early as 1912 and is still in daily use, and his legacy is significant in both popular culture and fine art – two areas his own career embraced so successfully. This legacy includes acknowledgements of his influence from people like Nick Park, creator of Wallace and Gromit; Mervyn Peake, author of the *Gormenghast* books; Rowland Emett, a cartoonist and whimsical inventor who is best remembered for his railway cartoons in *Punch*; conceptual architect C.J. Lim; and Thomas Heatherwick, designer of the 2012 Olympic Cauldron and the new Routemaster double-decker bus.

In the following chapters we shall see how this brilliant artist was called on to work for over 100 companies, advertising products as diverse as asbestos cement roofing, bread, carbon paper, bespoke tailoring, cigarettes and leather car seats. Advertising paid better than cartoons for magazines, and so the advertisers got the best of his contraptions and in many cases made sure that they were printed to the highest standards that technology would allow.

finer reproduction than magazines could offer. I think he would also have enjoyed the challenge of devising novel ways of promoting products over an extended series of drawings. This was especially true of his association with Connolly Bros, whose leather products he promoted in more than 200 drawings over a period of 20 years. On the negative side, it is

1

HEAVY ENGINEERING
AND MINING

Throughout the inter-war period the world economy was depressed, and in particular the coal industry was in decline, with frequent amalgamation of companies, culminating in nationalisation. There was therefore fierce competition for contracts. Also, at least at the beginning of the period, engineering companies were run by engineers who would have had an affinity with Heath Robinson's work, and Heath Robinson's reputation was such that to be associated with him was seen as a benefit in itself. No artist today has a comparable profile. His services, particularly in the areas of heavy engineering and mining, were very much in demand.

With their customers being either public bodies or large companies, the challenge for heavy engineering companies was to get their name in front of the employees responsible for purchasing and to keep it there. Heath Robinson's images captured the attention and were likely to be kept and possibly displayed in the office. Far from making the product advertised seem badly constructed or a joke, the very quality and ingenuity of his drawings were reassuring to the customer, while the gentle humour

11 A detail from *The Making of Asbestos Cement Roofing,* c.1930.

generated a sense of well-being and generosity towards the provider of such delights. A high-quality booklet would be sent to existing customers to keep them loyal, and might also be handed out to prospective customers at trade shows.

Another effective vehicle for the advertiser's message was a wall calendar, and one displaying Heath Robinson's inventive drawings would be bound to attract the attention of all who passed it. At a time before the invention of the ballpoint pen, clerical workers relied on fountain pens or old-fashioned dip pens, so blotting paper needed to be kept close at hand. A desk blotter with a new image each month was another way of keeping a company in the eye of the buyer.

The most favoured approach for such commissions was for Heath Robinson to visit the works to gain a full understanding of the processes involved in the manufacture of the product. He would then make a series of drawings showing 'Heath Robinson's view' of how it was done. This format was used to advertise cement, asbestos cement roofing products and many other things. For Booth's structural steel he varied the formula,

showing the positive difference that resulted from
the use of the company's products, while for 'Duroid'
road surfaces he devised a series of ingenious tests
to demonstrate to councillors and aldermen the
benefits that the product would bring to a local
authority area (figs 37–8).

Another alternative to showing the manufacturing
process was to take a humorous historical look
at an industry, and we see this deployed to good
effect in *The 'First' Colliery* (figs 41–5). These designs
for a calendar were commissioned in 1922 by
Fletcher, Burrows & Co. of Atherton in Lancashire.
They were reissued as a calendar by Lancashire
Associated Collieries in 1938 and later as postcards
by Manchester Collieries Ltd.

Individual pieces of machinery that were designed
for digging or flattening ground were already halfway
to being 'Heath Robinson' devices, so it must have
taken little imagination for the companies who
made such machines to use him to promote their
businesses. He was employed to dream up his own
outlandish versions of such contraptions as 'the
walking dragline', 'the grab-crane' or 'the skimmer'.

Many of those managing companies in the heavy
engineering or construction fields would have
served during the First World War. They would
have been familiar with Heath Robinson's wartime
cartoons and seen the similarity between many of
his inventions – such as the armoured corn-presser
(fig.12) – and their own products or processes. They
would also remember the positive effect that those
humorous drawings had in raising morale, and
would have wanted to harness that effect to market
their products or services.

13 'Digging the Raw Materials: Messrs G. & T. Earle's new patent combination action digger at work', from *The Wonders of Wilmington*, 1927.

CEMENT MAKING ON THE BANKS OF THE HUMBER

G. & T. Earle had been making cement in Hull, on the banks of the River Humber, since 1821 and occupied their Wilmington site in 1866. The company installed two rotary kilns in 1906, doubling the plant's capacity, and a third and fourth rotary kiln in 1913 and 1920 respectively. By 1925 they were producing 150,000 tonnes of cement a year (about 4.5 per cent of the total UK output). However, it was their marketing capability and excellent transport network that marked them out from their competitors. In 1912 they became a subsidiary of Associated Portland Cement Manufacturers Ltd, subsequently absorbed in Blue Circle Industries PLC, but they continued to operate as a separate entity until 1969.

Heath Robinson was engaged to work for the company in 1928 and produced a set of five large and intricate halftone illustrations of stages in the making of cement (figs 11 and 13–7). These were finely reproduced in a large-format book titled *The Wonders of Wilmington*. Earle's cement was marketed under the brand name 'Pelican', and this bird not only appeared on the cover of the book, but can be discovered observing proceedings in each of the drawings. The book proved popular, and when stocks were exhausted, Earle had postcards made of the illustrations to give to clients. The book was reproduced in a smaller format in 1949 as *Earle's Early Etchings*, and this version was reprinted by Blue Circle Industries in 1984.

14 'Working Overtime on the Slurry Mixing Tanks', from *The Wonders of Wilmington*, 1927.

15 'The Rotary Kilns where the Slurry is Calcined before Grinding', from *The Wonders of Wilmington*, 1927.

16 'Grinding and Packing Portland Cement', from *The Wonders of Wilmington*, 1927.

17 'Some Severe Tests to which Cement is Submitted at Wilmington', from *The Wonders of Wilmington*, 1927.

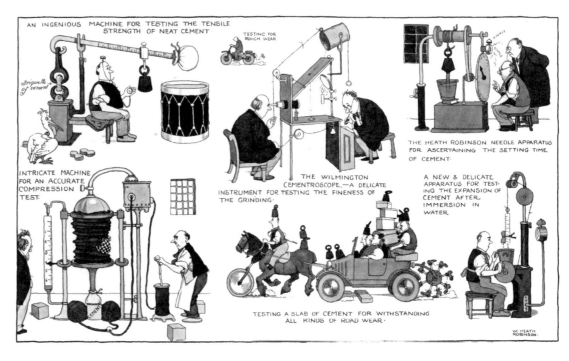

THE MAKING OF ASBESTOS CEMENT ROOFING

Asbestos Cement Building Products was a marketing organisation set up in 1929 to handle sales for Turner's Asbestos Cement Company based in Trafford Park, Manchester. The company had its own asbestos mines, including the largest in South Africa.

Heath Robinson was invited to visit the works in about 1930 and to make a number of drawings for a promotional book in which 'he portrayed the various processes of manufacture in his own inimitable way' (figs 18–22). The book was finely printed by photogravure on heavy, deckle-edged paper and tied in embossed card covers with a silk ribbon.

The directors were clearly delighted with Heath Robinson's drawings and made use of them in various ways. In July 1932 a report in the *Whitstable Times and Tankerton Press* of a lecture given to the Canterbury and District Ironmongers' Assistants' Association on 'Asbestos' records that:

A number of interesting lantern slides which were shown included views of the mines and quarries in various parts of the world and the uses of the asbestos cement products, concluding with a highly diverting series of Heath Robinson cartoons showing the alleged methods of mining and of producing asbestos goods.[1]

19 'A Patent Double-action Grinder for Mashing the Asbestos Fibre', from *The Making of Asbestos Cement Roofing*, c.1930.

20 'Efficient Plant for the Mixing of Treated Asbestos Fibre with Cement', from *The Making of Asbestos Cement Roofing*, c.1930.

21 'Powerful Machinery for Conveying the Mixture to the Cylindrical Sieves for Draining Off the Water, whence . . . a thin film is conveyed to the cylinder upon which the sheet is built, and this finally to the cutting machine', from *The Making of Asbestos Cement Roofing, c.*1930.

22 'An Interesting Afternoon in the Finishing Departments of an Asbestos Cement Factory', from *The Making of Asbestos Cement Roofing*, c.1930.

23 'Welded Structural Work. Mr W. Heath Robinson "Gilds the Lily"', from *Problems of a Structural Engineer*, c.1930.

24 'Drilling', from *Problems of a Structural Engineer*, c.1930.

DRILLING

A BETTER LIFE WITH STRUCTURAL STEEL

In about 1930 Heath Robinson was asked to provide illustrations for a promotional booklet for John Booth & Sons of Bolton who specialised in steel structures (figs 23–32). The booklet was titled *Problems of a Structural Engineer*. It had an introduction by the prominent humorist Ashley Sterne, and five of the full-page illustrations were in two parts, the upper part showing the problem and the remainder the solution provided by Booth Steelworks.

A second, more substantial booklet was produced in 1937. This used four of the full-page drawings from the first booklet together with three new drawings. There were also numerous photographs of steel structures, including the framework for the ill-fated Quarry Hill flats in Leeds. One of the largest modernist buildings in Europe, social problems and poor maintenance led to their demolition in 1978.

25 'How to Provide Suitable Accommodation and Comfort for Onlookers at a Football Match. The latest super all-steel football stand', from *Booth Steelwork*, c.1937.

26 'Re-housing a Weaving Shed so as to Eliminate the Forest of Columns and Provide Accommodation for Machinery and Workpeople', from *Problems of a Structural Engineer, c.*1930.

27 'High-speed Hilarity at Blackpool as Visualised by Mr W. Heath Robinson', from *Booth Steelwork*, c.1937.

28 'Extension of Business Premises without Disruption of Trade', from *Problems of a Structural Engineer*, c.1930.

29 'Building a Bridge without Interference with Vested Interests Already on the Site', from *Problems of a Structural Engineer, c.*1930.

30 'Mr Heath Robinson Suggests that Rebuilding is "child's play", it looks it!', from *Booth Steelwork, c.*1937.

31 'A Portable Electric Emery Wheel Grinder Fitted with Patent Balancer', from *Problems of a Structural Engineer, c.*1930.

32 'Building a Super Cinema in Rough Country', from *Problems of a Structural Engineer*, c.1930. A black-and-white version of this image was later printed in *Booth Steelwork*, c.1937 with the additional caption: 'Showing that the adaptability of Mr W. Heath Robinson's 'Steelwork' is equal to dealing with any difficulties presented by the site at the locality.'

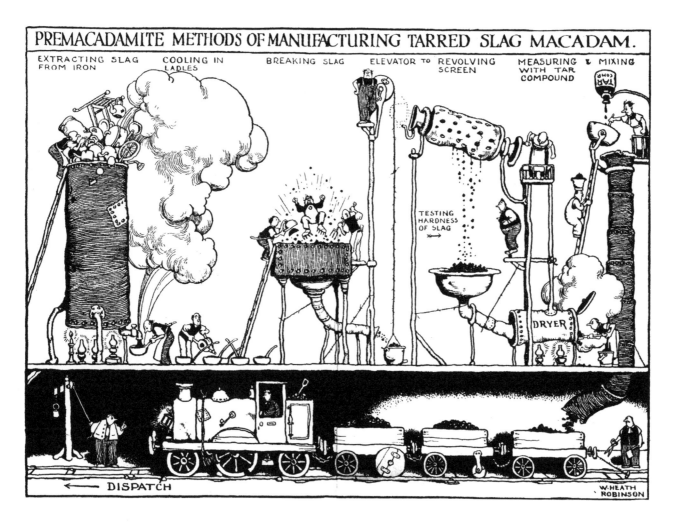

PREMACADAMITE METHODS OF MANUFACTURING TARRED SLAG MACADAM.

EXTRACTING SLAG FROM IRON · COOLING IN LADLES · BREAKING SLAG · ELEVATOR TO REVOLVING SCREEN · MEASURING & MIXING WITH TAR COMPOUND

TESTING HARDNESS OF SLAG →

DRYER

← DISPATCH

W. HEATH ROBINSON

33 'Premacadamite Methods of Manufacturing Tarred Slag Macadam', inside of Crow Catchpole & Co. Christmas card, undated (after 1921).

34 'Tar & Macadam', back and front of Crow Catchpole & Co. Christmas card, undated (after 1921).

BASSETTS LTD

In November 1921 Heath Robinson's agent A.E. Johnson was visited by the Managing Director of Bassetts Ltd who were makers of asphalt in Birmingham. They wanted a Christmas card 'to send out to road-surveyors and the like' (figs 33–4). The fee for the job was to be 30 guineas.

Johnson suggested that the front of the card should feature 'the first MacAdam i.e. a Scotch version of Adam, the first man, wearing a kilt made of fig leaves'. On the back page would be MacAdam and a Jack Tar toasting each other. The inside of the card was to be a typical Heath Robinson drawing of the manufacturing process. The design was subsequently used by Crow Catchpole & Co.

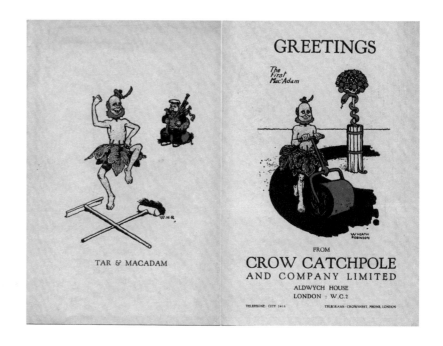

TAR & MACADAM

GREETINGS

The First MacAdam

FROM
CROW CATCHPOLE
AND COMPANY LIMITED
ALDWYCH HOUSE
LONDON : W.C.2

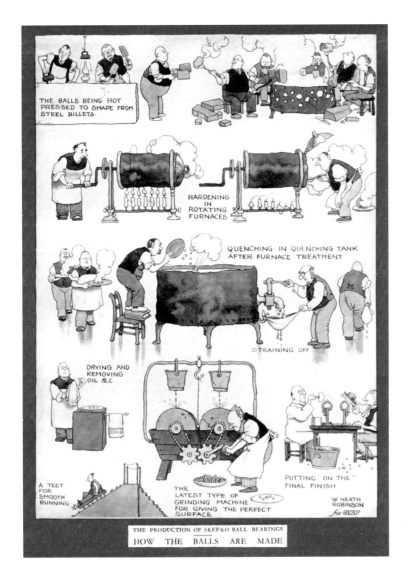

THE SKEFKO BALL BEARING COMPANY, LTD

SKF was founded in Gothenburg, Sweden, by Sven Wingqvist, inventor of the double-row self-aligning ball bearing. It opened offices in London under the name of the Skefko Ball Bearing Company Ltd in 1910 and the following year built a factory in Luton. They still operate from a much-enlarged site in Luton, making a wide range of high-technology products related to machinery with rotating components.

In 1926 the company turned to Heath Robinson to make two drawings for its Christmas promotion (figs 35–6). These were in the familiar style, showing Heath Robinson's idea of how the product was manufactured. As is usually the case, one can learn a great deal about the actual manufacturing process from Heath Robinson's conception of it. The two pictures were presented in a grey card folder 'With the compliments of SKF, Christmas, 1926'.

THE BENEFITS OF DUROID ROAD SURFACES

A set of 11 drawings were made in 1935 for desk blotters advertising Newton, Chambers & Co.'s Duroid road surfacing material (figs 37–8). These were designed for distribution to councillors and local government employees responsible for road maintenance.

Heath Robinson's humour is often directed at those who are pompous and take themselves too seriously, the officials and self-appointed experts. He also loved to invent unlikely methods of testing products. This commission offered him the perfect opportunity to develop a set of variations on these themes.

Desk blotters, by their nature, are ephemeral, and no examples of this set are known to survive. Fortunately, a few sets of proofs were printed on good-quality cartridge paper and issued in a plain black folder. The images here are taken from one such set. A number of the original drawings for the campaign were offered for sale by Chris Beetles Ltd in 2011.

37 Proofs for desk blotters, 1935.

38 (OPPOSITE) Proofs for desk blotters, 1935.

THE TEST FOR FREEDOM FROM BLEEDING AND PICKING UP

ORDINARY ROAD

DUROID

DEMONSTRATING THAT DUROID HOLDS BIG CHIPS ON A ROAD AFTER SPRAYING AND ROLLING

A DEMONSTRATION OF THE TENACITY OF DUROID MACADAM

BARFORD & PERKINS MOTOR ROLLERS

Barford & Perkins started making steam-driven agricultural machinery and rollers in the 1870s. They introduced petrol- and paraffin-fuelled machinery in 1904 and demonstrated the application of the internal combustion engine to rollers at the Darlington Show in 1920. Diesel rollers were introduced in 1927.

A little notebook with a celluloid cover was produced in 1931 (fig.39). The date and place of publication of the drawing of the WHY4 roller (fig.40) have not been traced, but both the name and design are pure Heath Robinson, down to the secretary's whisky and soda. Note that the roller is being used by the Why Not Tennis Club.

39 Miniature Celluloid-covered Notebook, 1931.

40 'The New Model WHY4 Roller' source untraced.

THE 'FIRST' COLLIERY

The Fletcher family first mined coal in Atherton, Lancashire in 1776. Abraham Burrows became a partner in the business in 1872. The company was a good employer as well as having a reputation for good management, and in the 1870s it built homes at Hindsford and the model village at Howe Bridge for its workers. A public bathhouse, shops and a social club were part of the village. The workers, some of them women who sorted coal on the pit brow screens, were provided with hampers or turkeys at Christmas by the company. In 1927 Robert Burrows proposed a merger of several local colliery companies operating west of Manchester, including the Atherton Collieries. As a result Manchester Collieries was formed in 1929. In turn, when the coal industry was nationalised in 1947, Manchester Collieries became part of the National Coal Board.

Heath Robinson's agent A.E. Johnson was approached by Fletcher, Burrows & Co. in October 1921 to know whether Heath Robinson could do four drawings for a calendar that they contemplated issuing the following year (figs 42–5). The approach had been inspired by the booklet that had recently been produced for the Port of Manchester Warehouses. Johnson replied quoting a price of 60 guineas for black and white or 100 guineas for colour. The colliery opted for black and white and invited Heath Robinson to visit the works. He duly visited and prepared rough sketches of his proposed designs which were sent to Burrows for approval in early November. They were given due consideration and in January Heath Robinson heard that they were extremely pleased with them and had only one minor request for an alteration. He also received a request for an additional drawing for a cover sheet, originally to be printed in two colours, black and red or black and orange, but this idea was quickly abandoned in favour of a plain line drawing (fig.41). The calendar was printed in March and Heath Robinson expressed his satisfaction with the finished product.

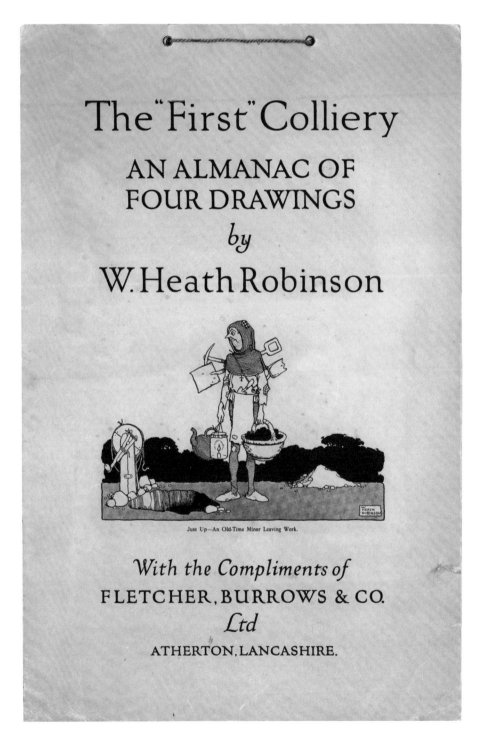

41 Calendar cover with the drawing 'Just Up – An Old-Time Miner Leaving Work', 1922.

42 'The Pit Head', from *The 'First' Colliery* calendar, 1922.

43 'The Pit (sectional view)', from *The 'First' Colliery* calendar, 1922.

44 'Screening and Picking Coal', from *The 'First' Colliery* calendar, 1922.

45 'A Busy Day in the Washery', from *The 'First' Colliery* calendar, 1922.

46 'An Early Form of the Walking Dragline . . .', from *The Gentle Art of Excavating*, c.1938.

THE GENTLE ART OF EXCAVATING

Ruston-Bucyrus Ltd was an engineering company formed in 1930. It was jointly owned by Ruston & Hornsby based in Lincoln, and an American company called Bucyrus-Erie. Already the leading British manufacturer of excavating machinery, the company quickly expanded its range to include skimmers, walking draglines and grab cranes. Heath

Robinson was commissioned to visit the works and make a series of drawings to illustrate a promotional booklet titled *The Gentle Art of Excavating* (figs 46–50). This was published with a whimsical text purporting to be written by Heath Robinson, although how much of it he wrote, if any, is not clear. The date of publication is not given, but inclusion of the walking dragline suggests sometime after 1935.

47 'A New Type of Shovel Removing the Top Soil from a Bluff in the Cotswold Hills', from *The Gentle Art of Excavating*, c.1938.

48 'A New Multi-movement Drag Shovel . . .',
from *The Gentle Art of Excavating*, c.1938.

49 'The Beginning of a Garden Suburb – Excavating a New Road with a Specially Designed Skimmer', from *The Gentle Art of Excavating*, c.1938.

50 'The Latest Type of Grab Crane Clearing out a Small Pond on Hampstead Heath', from *The Gentle Art of Excavating*, c.1938.

HOW BAYLISS, JONES & BAYLISS LTD MAKE WROUGHT-IRON FENCING AND GATES

The company that became Bayliss, Jones & Bayliss Ltd was founded in 1826 when William Bayliss established the Victoria Works in Cable Street, Wolverhampton. Here he made iron products including sheep hurdles, railings, gates, stable fittings, ornamental ironwork and chains for mining and shipping. In the early 1900s the firm's two main areas of production were ornamental fencing and components for railways. From the 1920s the company seems to have concentrated more on the fencing, railing and general ornamental ironwork side. They were hit hard in the great slump of 1929–30 but recovered strongly from the mid 1930s, which were their most successful years. It was in the 1930s that Heath Robinson was employed to advertise their fencing and gates in *Punch* and other magazines (figs 51–2).

51 'The Making of "Bayliss Nibal" Fencing', published in *Punch Almanack* for 1933.

52 'How Wrought Iron Gates are Wrought', published in *Punch* Summer Number 1932.

2

FOOD AND DRINK

In the first half of 1915, Heath Robinson was commissioned to make a set of six drawings showing stages in the making of Johnnie Walker whisky. The drawings illustrate testing casks, designing the label, squaring the bottles, filtering the liquor, filling bottles and testing the whisky. The approach to the drawings is similar to six cartoons that he had made for *The Sketch* some three years earlier showing the editing and production of that magazine. Heath Robinson had made pen-and-wash drawings of imagined manufacturing processes as early as December 1908 when *Kippering Herrings by the side of the River Yare* (see fig.2), the first of his 'Great British Industries' series, appeared in *The Sketch*, but this was the first time that such drawings had been commissioned for advertising. The company still owns the original drawings, but there is no record of the format in which they were first published. The fact that there are six drawings might suggest a calendar or booklet, but they might equally have appeared as a sequence of magazine advertisements.

The widespread demand for Heath Robinson to show how a product is made probably stems from the occasion in 1921 when he was asked by John Mackintosh & Sons of Halifax to provide the first in a series of cartoons by famous artists showing how and where they imagine Toffee de Luxe is made. Heath Robinson called his drawing *A Half Hour in Toffee Town* and, with a series of six small line drawings in a single frame, showed the various stages in the toffee-making process (fig.64). These included boiling, cooling, shaping, covering with chocolate, counting and testing, all conducted by solemn little men operating typical Heath Robinson machinery. Mackintosh's were delighted with the drawing. H. Mackintosh, the Managing Director, wrote to Heath Robinson: 'Since your drawing was placed before us by our Agents, Messrs T B Browne Limited, we have had many a good laugh over same. Knowing the real factory, we can appreciate your caricature all the more.' On Saturday 1 October 1921, the whole of the front page of the *Daily Mail* and several other daily papers were occupied by Heath Robinson's depiction of Toffee Town, and the drawing subsequently appeared in reduced form in other periodicals and in a Mackintosh's booklet.

The depiction of an unconventional history of the product was a frequently used approach to

53 Detail from 'The First Steam Mill', from *An Unconventional History of Hovis*, 1926.

advertising work, being a useful alternative to the manufacturing process, or in some cases an adjunct to it. Perhaps the most complete and satisfying advertising booklet adopting a historical approach was *An Unconventional History of Hovis*, published in 1926. In its 24 pages was recorded the history of Hovis baking, from the discovery of wheat in prehistoric times, through the first windmill and the first steam mill, to modern methods of production and testing (figs 54–63).

The historical approach was also used for Sandy Macdonald's Scotch whisky (fig.71). It is interesting to note that, while toffees are tested on schoolboys and sugar on babies, the quality of the whisky is judged by its effect on an ancient.

Some of Heath Robinson's most pleasing coloured work was for biscuit manufacturers. He designed a tin incorporating 'The Heath Robinson Golf Course' for Peek Frean (fig.67), and a card insert showing 'Mr Heath Robinson's conception of a modern biscuit plant' for William Crawford & Sons (fig.68).

AN UNCONVENTIONAL HISTORY OF HOVIS

Hovis is a particular brand of flour. The Hovis process was patented in 1886 by a miller called Richard 'Stoney' Smith. The Macclesfield firm of S. Fitton & Sons Ltd developed the brand, milling the flour and selling it along with Hovis-branded baking tins to other bakers. Its name was coined in 1890 by Herbert Grime in a national competition set by Fittons to find a trading name for their patent flour which was rich in wheat germ. It derives from the Latin phrase *hominis vis* – 'the strength of man'. From 1892 the brand was heavily promoted by various forms of advertising.

Heath Robinson's 'unconventional history' was published in 1926. He had first used the 'historical'

54 'The Discovery of Wheat', from *An Unconventional History of Hovis*, 1926.

approach in an advertising commission in the calendar that he designed for Fletcher, Burrows & Co. in 1921 showing how a mediaeval mine might have operated (see figs 41–5). This time he was given the space to track the development of baking from the Stone Age to the 20th century (figs 54–62).

55 'Primitive Methods of Cutting and Threshing the Wild Corn', from *An Unconventional History of Hovis*, 1926.

56 'The First Millstones. Some prehistoric methods of grinding and pounding the hard corn for convenience in making cakes etc. etc', from *An Unconventional History of Hovis*, 1926.

57 'The Landing of the Romans in Ancient Britain', from *An Unconventional History of Hovis*, 1926.

58 'Ancient Britons, having received some useful tips from the Romans, soon got into the way of baking their own cakes', from *An Unconventional History of Hovis*, 1926.

59 'The First Windmill', from *An Unconventional History of Hovis*, 1926.

60 'The First Steam Mill', from *An Unconventional History of Hovis*, 1926.

In 1928 a final illustration from the book also appeared, in colour, in *Punch, Tatler, Good Housekeeping* and a number of other magazines (fig.63). It satirises the type of advertisements that try to convince the prospective customer that if they buy product X their life will be transformed, but does so with such good humour that one almost believes that with Hovis this might just be true.

The illustration, which was also published in full colour as a magazine advertisement, contrasts the thin, sickly and fractious family that does not eat Hovis with the plump, healthy and contented inhabitants of 'The Hovis Home'. The differences extend to the cat, dog and caged bird, and even to the family's pot plants.

61 'Busy Times in the Hovis Testing Laboratories', from *An Unconventional History of Hovis*, 1926.

62 'Interior of Modern Bakery', from *An Unconventional History of Hovis*, 1926.

63 'Hovis, the Bread of Health', published in *The Sketch* Christmas Number 1926; *Punch Almanack* for 1927, and *Nash's Pall Mall Magazine*, January 1927.

MACKINTOSH'S TOFFEE DE LUXE
— W. Heath Robinson's impression of Toffee Town.

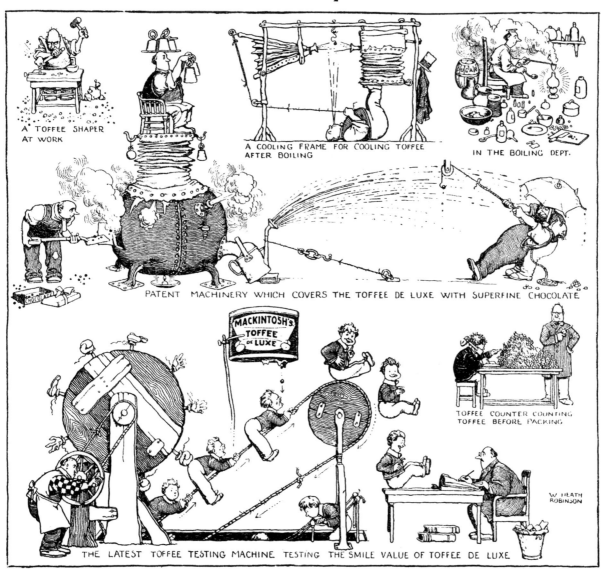

A TOFFEE SHAPER AT WORK

A COOLING FRAME FOR COOLING TOFFEE AFTER BOILING

IN THE BOILING DEPT.

PATENT MACHINERY WHICH COVERS THE TOFFEE DE LUXE WITH SUPERFINE CHOCOLATE

TOFFEE COUNTER COUNTING TOFFEE BEFORE PACKING

THE LATEST TOFFEE TESTING MACHINE TESTING THE SMILE VALUE OF TOFFEE DE LUXE

64 'Heath Robinson's Impression of Toffee Town', which on Saturday 1 October 1921 filled the whole of the front page of the *Daily Mail*.

MACKINTOSH'S TOFFEE

Between October 1921 and March 1922, Mackintosh's bought seven full-pages in national daily newspapers and commissioned the best-known comic artists to contribute drawings on the subject of 'Toffee Town' and their imagined view of it. The campaign ran for six months, with one front page a month in each of the *Daily Mail*, *Daily Express*, *Daily News*, *Daily Mirror*, *Daily Sketch* and several provincial newspapers. This was an enormous scheme for the early 1920s and cost approximately £25,000. For the first cartoon, Harold Mackintosh commissioned Heath Robinson, an indication of the high regard in which he was held (fig.64). Other artists included H.M. Bateman, Mabel Lucie Attwell, 'Fougasse' (Cyril Kenneth Bird) and Bruce Bairnsfather.

A COMMISSION FROM BELGIUM

Heath Robinson's work was familiar to European audiences from his First World War cartoons, which were reproduced in magazines in France, Portugal and elsewhere. In February 1922 Heath Robinson's agent was approached by a representative of Stiff & Co., starch manufacturers. He wanted a series of advertisements on the lines of the Mackintosh's toffee one. A.E. Johnson quoted a fee of 40 guineas

65 'The Making of Remy Macaroni', poster, c.1922.

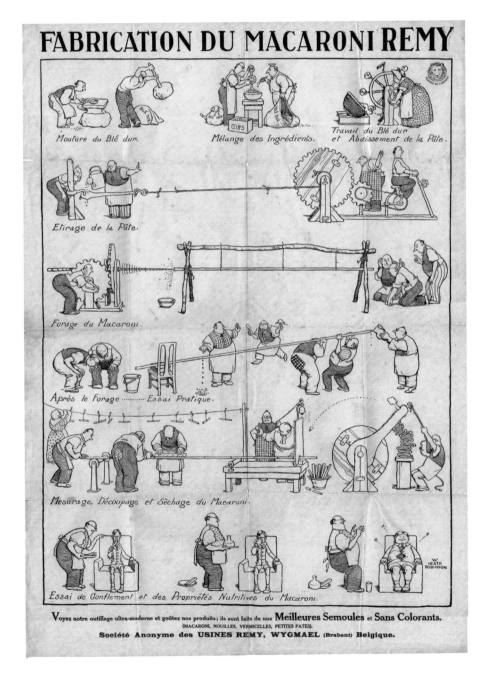

(per picture), with possible reductions for a series of six or 12. He reported that: 'after chewing the cud he writes to say that they are prepared to order from you one drawing to advertise Remy's Macaroni.' He reminded Heath Robinson that he had some years before designed a poster for Remy's Starch [not seen]. He went on: 'The writer of the letter, one Monette (a quite pleasant Frenchman speaking perfectly good English) would like to come down and meet you with a view to explaining to you the manufacturing processes.'

A rough sketch was made, and on 24 March Johnson reported that Monette seemed very pleased with it and was sending it to his friends. Their comments were received on 30 March. They were very pleased with the sketches but requested some modifications to bring the subjects more closely into line with their manufacturing processes:

(1) It is important to emphasise the <u>hardness</u> of the wheat, and they would like the first sketch of all to be something representing a supposed process of crushing this very hard wheat. I suggested to Monette that you might perhaps do a sketch of a very brawny person with an immense sledge-hammer crushing the hard wheat on a blacksmith's anvil. This, he says, is exactly the kind of subject they want.
(2) The second sketch should be 'Mixing the Ingredients' for which your existing rough is perfectly satisfactory, subject to three small modifications. These are:-
a. The word 'semolina' should be deleted from the barrel on the left.
b. A box or basket of eggs should be substituted for the jug of milk in front of the table.
c. The bags on the right should be labelled 'Hard Wheat' not 'Whole Wheat'.
In place of the old woman with roller [sic] pin for the subject 'Kneading the Paste' they would like some sort of comic kneading machine . . . They would like to keep the old woman, but she ought to be seen turning the handle of some sort of machine in which the paste is being automatically kneaded.

The HEATH ROBINSON GOLF COURSE

Packed with PEEK FREAN'S BISCUITS

And so the letter goes on for another page and a half. On 5 March Johnson acknowledged receipt of an amended sketch which the clients were happy with, and on 27 April the finished drawing was delivered (fig.65). On 10 May Johnson reported that it had met with complete approval. It was used for press advertisements and also made into a small poster.

PEEK FREAN'S BISCUITS

Peek Frean & Co. was founded in 1857 and moved into their purpose-built factory in Bermondsey, south-east London, in 1866. They produced a wide range of biscuits there until 1989. They were the originators of such well-known varieties as Garibaldi, Marie and Bourbon.

Novelty biscuit tins were a popular way of promoting their wares, and one of the most elaborate was the 'Heath Robinson Golf Course' design, produced in about 1925, which included a golf game inside (not by Heath Robinson) (figs 66–7).

66 The original watercolour made for the Peek Frean's biscuit tin, 328 × 483 mm (12½ × 19 in). (Photo courtesy of Chris Beetles Ltd)

67 The Peek Frean biscuit tin with the golf game inside.

CRAWFORD'S BISCUITS

Crawford's started making biscuits in Edinburgh in 1813. They prided themselves on always having the latest and best machinery and methods for making their biscuits. The company was acquired by United Biscuits in 1960, but production continues under the Crawford's name.

Mr. Heath Robinson's Conception of a Modern Biscuit Plant was commissioned in 1933 for use in press advertisements and for cards to be included in packets of biscuits (fig.68).

68 An original card from a tin of Crawford's biscuits.

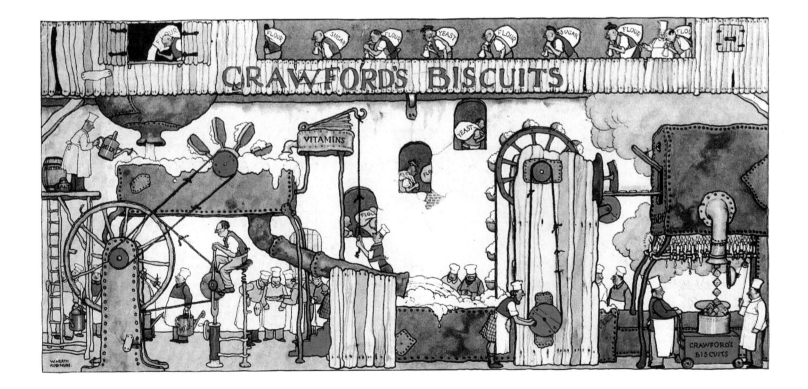

69 'The Finest Thirst I Ever Knew — the thirst that saved a life', published in *Punch*, 1925.

70 'It's Thirsty Work', published in *Punch*, 1926.

PRESS ADVERTISEMENTS FOR BARCLAY'S LAGER

In 1925 Barclay, Perkins & Co. ran an advertising campaign for their lager under the title 'The Finest Thirst I Ever Knew (A Symposium by Eminent Artists)' (fig.69). It appeared as a series of half-page advertisements in *Punch,* and other artists employed in the campaign included Lawson Wood, Aubrey Hammond, J.H. Dowd and Harold Earnshaw. Heath Robinson's contribution was to show 'the thirst that saved a life'. The drawing *It's thirsty work* was published in *Punch* the following year (fig.70).

Barclay's Lager was produced at the Anchor Brewery in Southwark which had been brewing beer since 1616. It was offered as 'light or dark'. Barclay, Perkins & Co. merged with Courage in 1955.

71 Magazine advertisement for Sandy Macdonald Scotch Whisky, published in *The Sketch* Christmas Number 1922.

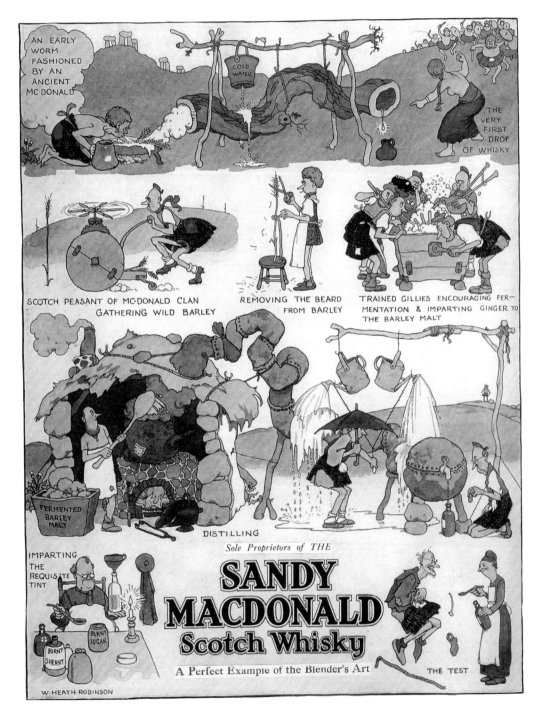

TRADITIONAL METHODS OF MAKING WHISKY

Sandy Macdonald Scotch whisky was produced at the Glendullan Distillery which opened in 1898. It was owned by William Williams and Sons who in 1919 changed their name to Macdonald, Greenlees & Williams (Distillers) Ltd. The distillery was located in Dufftown on the River Fiddich. In 1926 this distillery also became part of Distillers Company. Sandy Macdonald seems to have disappeared as a brand in the UK in the 1930s, but was still being marketed in South America in the mid-1980s.

Heath Robinson clearly enjoyed the commission to make a full-page coloured illustration promoting the company's whisky, which probably involved a trip to the distillery. As with Hovis, he adopted the historical approach (fig.71). With one exception, his humour never involved poking fun at racial stereotypes. That exception was the Scots, who were regarded as fair game, but even with them there is always gentleness and affection in the parody.

THE MAKING OF JOHNNIE WALKER WHISKY

John 'Johnnie' Walker started selling whisky from the family grocery shop in Kilmarnock in about 1825. The distinctive square bottle was introduced in 1870, which resulted in fewer breakages and more efficient packing. The whisky, which had been known as 'Walker's Kilmarnock', was renamed 'Johnnie Walker' in 1908. The employment of Heath Robinson in 1915 represented a departure from the company's usual advertising style, which featured the figure of a dapper striding man created by the artist Tom Browne in 1909 and the slogan 'Born 1820 – Still going strong'. Johnnie Walker became part of Distillers Company in 1925 which was taken over by Guinness in 1986 and which in turn became part of Diageo in 1997.

Heath Robinson's series of drawings showing the making of Johnnie Walker whisky were made during the First World War, but it is not known where they were first published (figs 72–7). However, the company reprinted them in 1987.

72 'The Johnnie Walker Cask Experts Testing the Soundness of a Cask', 1915, reprinted 1987.

73 'Designing the Well-Known Get-up of Johnnie Walker in the Johnnie Walker Studios', 1915, reprinted 1987.

74 'Squaring the Johnnie Walker Bottles', 1915, reprinted 1987.

75 'In the Filtering Vaults at Kilmarnock', 1915, reprinted 1987.

76 'In the Johnnie Walker Filling Cellars', 1915, reprinted 1987.

77 'The Johnnie Walker Experts Testing Whisky Samples with the Patent Testing Dial in the Sample Room', 1915, reprinted 1987.

IMPRESSIONS OF A WELL-KNOWN SHERRY WORKS

Display panels were produced using a Heath Robinson design to advertise Domecq's sherry (fig.78). Commissioned by importers Luis Gordon & Sons, they had a tin-plate backing and were laminated. They were designed to stand on the counter in an off-licence. It is not known when these were made, but the style suggests the early 1930s. Heath Robinson adopts the standard 'how I imagine the manufacturing process' approach, here enlivened by the use of colour.

There was a variant of the main design that advertised 'Magnola' sherry.

79 'The Cropwell Herd of Pedigree Middle White Pigs Wins Prizes', probably 1922, pen, ink and monochrome watercolour, 380 × 260 mm (15 × 10¼ in).

A PRIZE HERD

Henry Smith of The Grove, Cropwell Butler, Nottinghamshire, appears as a member of the National Pig Breeders Association in the very first herd-book published in 1885. By 1910 he was a member of the Council and also the Auditor. By 1920 the Cropwell herd of Middle White pigs was in the name of Cuthbert C. Smith, who was enjoying a degree of success at agricultural shows. In October 1922 he approached Heath Robinson's agent A.E. Johnson to ask for prices for a design for a calendar. Surviving correspondence from Johnson to Heath Robinson reveals that he was quoted 30 guineas for a single subject in black and white or 35 guineas for one in colour. For a series of small sketches, 40 guineas or 50 guineas respectively. This was too much for Smith, so Johnson went back with an offer of 25 guineas for a single subject in colour, which was accepted. Smith sent photographs of the pigs and some suggestions for subject matter. A rough drawing in black and white was sent in early December. A proof was ready just before Christmas. At this point the trail of letters runs out. No copy of the published calendar has been located, and we just have the two drawings, which may relate to the 1922 commission (figs 79–80).

80 'The Ideal Pig Farm', probably 1922, pen, ink and monochrome watercolour, 410 × 305 mm (16⅛ × 12 in).

OXO

At the beginning of January 1921, William Heath Robinson's younger brother George approached his agent A.E. Johnson to enquire about the cost of a 10 × 8-inch (25 × 20-centimetre) colour drawing, the cost to cover the original and all rights. Johnson quoted 50 guineas and although the client 'were rather snorting over this figure', said that Heath Robinson 'could not very well do it for less'. The client, who was Oxo Ltd, did accept the figure and asked for a meeting. Heath Robinson was not enamoured with their initial ideas and suggested a drawing on the manufacture of Oxo. They wrote back on 25 January saying:

Although such an idea is excellent for many commodities, we are afraid that it is not at all suitable for Oxo. We hope, therefore that you will reconsider the matter of our suggestion.

May we again outline what we desire – we must have two white billiard balls and the rest making the word OXO perhaps somewhat enlarged. Then we think you could show very humorous drawings of the lookers-on making and drinking Oxo in different ways. There could be funny-shaped kettles, and spirit stoves, and perhaps a pipe, leading from the rooms above, and a man putting an Oxo Cube into another's mouth, and I am sure that other incidents will at once be suggested to you by your wonderful imagination.

It could be called – 'Watching an Exciting Game' or 'Waiting for their Cue', or 'Keeping their nerves steady during an Exciting Game', or something like that.

We feel sure that you could make an amusing picture on these lines while keeping Oxo well in the foreground.

We shall be very glad if you could see your way to reconsider your decision and meet our wishes in regard to this matter.

Heath Robinson made a rough sketch along the lines that they suggested. It did not meet with their approval, and a second sketch was prepared on the understanding that they would pay 5 guineas for it if the project was abandoned. This was sent on 7 February. Johnson comments that 'if they are not satisfied with this, we must come to the conclusion that they are hopeless'. It

was well received and a finished drawing was submitted in mid-March. Oxo wrote back: 'It is very excellent and we hope to make good use of this in the future.' However, that was not the end of the story. On 6 June Heath Robinson received a letter from Oxo stating:

Having had various opinions on the showcard, 'The Oxo Break,' which we are returning to you, there appears to be from our point of view one alteration which is necessary before we can put it out. The tank near the window containing the two handles we would like altered.

We are sending to you a photograph of the Oxo urn which we suggest might better take its place . . . Will you kindly make this alteration and let us have the design back at your earliest convenience.

Heath Robinson wrote back on 12 June. That letter is lost, but Oxo wrote again the next day:

We thank you for your letter of the 12th inst and I think you will understand the delicacy with which we have to approach the public in regard to illustrating Oxo in tanks or cisterns, and on this point we hold quite a definite opinion.

We quite agree with you that it would be better to have a more ornamental receptacle instead of the large tank.

In place of the small cistern by all means put an Oxo bottle, though something in the nature of our lighthouse urn we think would be preferable.

The water boiler, by which you mean, we pre-sume, the lighthouse urn would be a silver colour. The pump engine on top of the small cistern is not so much criticised as the cistern itself, but it suggests beer rather than Oxo, and perhaps a tap, or some-thing similar would be better.

Many thanks for the trouble you are taking in the matter.

Here the trail ends. One must assume that the show card was amended as requested and was used, but no example of it is known to survive. It was not until 1941 that Heath Robinson worked for Oxo again, this time using a variant of his original suggestion (fig.81).

81 'An Idea for Producing More Oxo to Meet Wartime Needs', published in *My Home*, November 1941.

82 'How we make sure there are 2,400 drops of flavour in every 9d bottle of Yorkshire Relish', postcard, 1923.

83 Display advertisement for A. & W. Smith & Co. Ltd, date unknown.

YORKSHIRE RELISH

Yorkshire Relish was a piquant sauce made from pickled fruits produced in Leeds by Goodall, Backhouse & Co. It was first made in the 1830s and continued in production in Leeds until the 1960s. A version is still produced in Ireland.

Heath Robinson was asked to make a drawing advertising the product in December 1922. This was to be in two colours and to focus on the manufacturer's claim that there are 2,400 drops in every bottle. The price for the drawing was 40 guineas. Having seen a rough sketch, the clients asked that there should be 'a regretful and tearful procession of old men bearing away rejected bottles that have been proved to contain only 2399¾ drops'. Their other request was for a counter showing the day's total production. The drawing was certainly used on postcards (fig.82) and probably also for press advertisements.

STAGES IN THE SUGAR REFINING PROCESS

In 1837 brothers Andrew and William Smith, millwrights, formed a partnership under the name A. & W. Smith & Co, millwrights and machine engineers. Their first machine was a steam-driven sugar mill for Tobago, West Indies. In 1855 they moved into the Eglinton Engine Works in Tradeston, Glasgow. As well as producing sugar-refining machinery, the firm produced bridges and structural steelwork for locomotive sheds and buildings. Railway wagons and weighbridges were also a speciality. In the 20th century, the inter-war period saw the sugar machine industry struggle in the general depression. Most of the sugar-producing areas were equipped with relatively new machinery with a long life expectancy, so the stable demand for sugar meant little work for machinery builders. It was probably at this time that Heath Robinson's help was enlisted. The relatively large image (fig.83), produced photographically and backed with card, would have been made in small numbers and used at trade shows.

3

CLOTHING AND TEXTILES

One of the first requests for advertising work after the First World War came from the Lancashire cotton-manufacturing firm of Horrockses, Crewdson & Co. who required three large drawings showing 'the manufacture of cotton fabrics according to Heath Robinson – the famous humorist' (figs 84 and 110–12). These were to be published at the front of a desk diary for 1922 under the heading 'How it is done!'. Particularly attractive is the idea of cotton spinning being performed exclusively by spinsters of a certain age.

Heath Robinson always paid great attention to the details of clothing in his drawings, to the extent that it is possible to date some of them from the fashions, particularly in hats. It was therefore appropriate that he should be called on to provide publicity material for leading gentlemen's outfitters. The first such commission was a drawing made for the Regent Street tailor Hector Powe sometime before 1925 called *The History of a Pair of Trousers*. This is described by Percy Bradshaw in *Art in Advertising* and was published in *The Pow-Wow*, the company's customer magazine.[1] A later drawing, published in the same magazine in 1932,

showed Heath Robinson's ideas of Hector Powe service.

Similar in style is the set of drawings made for a New York outfitter, the Rogers Peet Company, for a small portfolio entitled *Some Trade Secrets Revealed* (figs 103–9). As well as the inevitable 'how the product is tested' drawing, the portfolio includes clever plays on the names of some of Rogers Peet's product lines. Highlanders are shown rounding up mist for their lightweight 'Scotch Mist' tweed, and their 'So-light' hats are weighed against a feather. The ideas from this set were enlarged upon in the UK in the booklet *Behind the Scenes at Moss Bros* in 1936 (figs 85–94).

Another part of the trade that made good use of Heath Robinson's talents was dry-cleaning and laundry. Turnbulls of Hawick in Scotland were a well-known company of dry cleaners who, with a countrywide network of agents, provided a specialist dry-cleaning and dyeing service using postal and rail parcel services. They published a quarterly magazine for their clients and between 1929 and 1931 it included a double-page drawing showing Heath Robinson's view of some aspect of their business (figs 98–102). Customers could

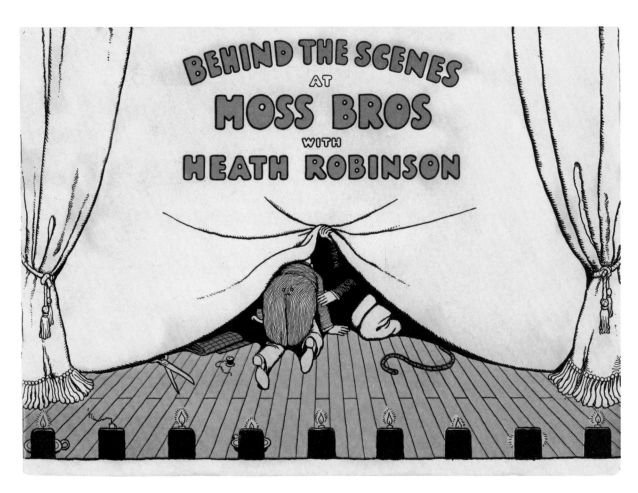

request reproductions of these drawings suitable for framing.

A more ephemeral business was that of silver fox farming. To encourage potential clients, a Mr T. Melross published a large book bound in art vellum and with illustrations by Heath Robinson, H.M. Bateman and others extolling the benefits of investing in his Nithsdale silver fox farm. An added incentive for investors was free access to 4,000 acres of grouse moor and to salmon fishing on the Nithsdale estate. Heath Robinson also contributed a cartoon to *Fur Farming* magazine showing his idea of how the foxes are fed.

BEHIND THE SCENES AT MOSS BROS

Moss Bros is a menswear company established by Moses Moss in London's Covent Garden in 1851. He sold second-hand clothing with the motto 'Sell only the best stuff, give only the best service'. He expanded the business by buying surplus stock from Savile Row tailors and by making up suits from remnants of fabric. The business moved to larger premises in nearby King Street in 1881. In 1894 Moses died, leaving the business to two of his sons, Alfred and George. Within five years the shop had been rebuilt and the Moss Bros name stood proudly over the door. The well-known hire service started in 1897 when Alfred lent evening wear to a friend, an impoverished singer, to enable him to work. The military clothing department developed after the Boer War and a saddlery department was added in the basement at King Street in the 1920s. In 1936, to celebrate a significant expansion of their Covent Garden premises, a substantial Heath Robinson booklet was sent to all of their account customers (figs 85–94). N.B. The captions are not Heath Robinson's.

86 'The Staff of our Olfactorium are all Men of International Repute. They are insured at Lloyd's for many thousands of pounds against the common cold', from *Behind The Scenes at Moss Bros . . .*, 1936.

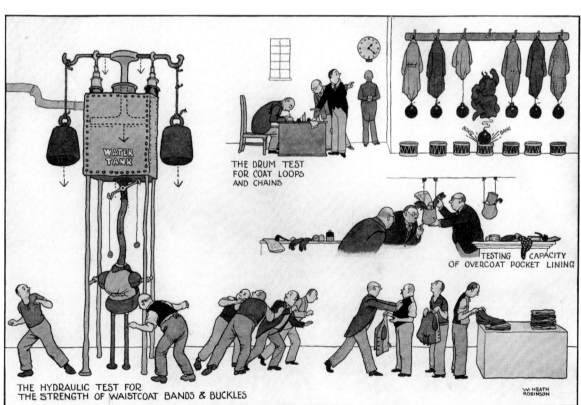

87 'The Man Responsible for the Strength of our Coat Loops has Recently Been Consulted by the Builders of a Famous Suspension Bridge', from *Behind The Scenes at Moss Bros . . .*, 1936.

88 'MOSS BROS. *de luxe* . . . Our emporium is exactly like this except for the palms, fountains . . .', from *Behind The Scenes at Moss Bros . . .*, 1936

89 'Those Week-end Cottages are all very well, but most of us like a little more luxury in our country seat', from *Behind The Scenes at Moss Bros . . .*, 1936.

90 '. . . pillars, stage, staircase, etc., etc. . . . But really – it's a very comfortable place in which to choose a suit', from *Behind The Scenes at Moss Bros . . .*, 1936.

91 'Arms and the man present no terrors to our students once they have taken their third degree at our Academy of Salesmanship', from *Behind The Scenes at Moss Bros . . .*, 1936.

92 'This is not quite the shape of things to come at MOSS BROS. . . . But we really have the Builders in – actually working', from *Behind The Scenes at Moss Bros . . .*, 1936.

93 'Last December our Christmas delivery in Mayfair was mistaken for a fog. Our aim is so sure that we can drop your new top-hat accurately on to your head', from *Behind The Scenes at Moss Bros . . .*, 1936.

MOSS BROS. & C⁰ L^{TD}

Naval, Military, R.A.F. General Outfitters & Saddlers

of COVENT GARDEN

(CORNER OF KING STREET
& BEDFORD STREET)
LONDON
W.C. 2

TELEPHONE
TEMPLE BAR 4477
(PRIVATE BRANCH EXCHANGE)

TELEGRAMS
PARSEE RAND
LONDON

ESTABLISHED 1881.

T.C. Whitehead Esq.,
Westbury House,
West Meon,
HANTS.

28th
March
1936.

Dear Sir,

Heath Robinson has got quite beyond our control!

It is amazing how he has contrived to distort the sober efforts of a firm that is striving to give customers the best possible, into weird contraptions which we don't know whether to describe as absurdly plausible or plausibly absurd.

Nevertheless he has weaved his whimsical web from a pattern of fact, and in one instance especially has departed hardly at all from the literal truth.

When he devoted a page to proposed building additions, he didn't know that such a project was about to begin.

We hope, with all due modesty, that it will occasion no surprise to you to learn that we can only continue to accommodate our customers comfortably by adding 50% more space.

Yours faithfully,
Moss Bros. & Co. Ltd.,

H.n.Moss

CCG/GC.

Director.

94 The letter that accompanied the Moss Bros booklet, to a Hampshire customer. Westbury House was a preparatory school in 1936.

95 'Some Interesting Processes in an Up-to-date Bleach Works', published in the *Manchester Guardian Commercial*, 30 June 1927.

BLEACHING AND FINISHING

Twenty-one companies engaged in the bleaching and finishing of cotton goods in the Manchester area commissioned a drawing which appeared in the *Manchester Guardian Commercial* newspaper on 30 June 1927 (fig.95). The accompanying text read:

> The undermentioned firms have been particularly fortunate in securing the services of Mr Heath Robinson to delineate in his inimitable style with a certain degree of accuracy the various processes of the trade, which will no doubt be interesting to merchants and users of Bleached Cotton Goods. The machines illustrated are provisionally protected, and any infringement of same will be dealt with the utmost rigour of the law.

THE GREAT NORTHERN LAUNDRY

The Great Northern Laundry was located in Finsbury Park, North London, close to where Heath Robinson was born. In the early 1920s they commissioned Heath Robinson to make a series of two-colour drawings promoting the modern methods and machinery that they employed (figs 96–7). On the back of one card they say that: 'The excellent value of this low-priced service is due to the up-to-date machinery used (even more up-to-date than Heath Robinson's idea on the back of this card)' (fig.97). This card was posted on 1 May 1923 to Mrs Huson at 21, Southwood Avenue, Highgate, N6. The Husons were longstanding friends of the Robinsons, having been neighbours in Hatch End, Pinner, between 1908 and 1911, and were to become neighbours again in about 1930 when Heath Robinson moved to the next-door-but-one house in Highgate.

The Heath Robinson Series of Laundry Impressions—No. 1.

THE COLLECTOR CALLS

Prompt Collection and Delivery is a feature of our Service (see back).

96 'Prompt Collection and Delivery is a Feature of our Service', postcard, 1923.

The Heath Robinson Series of Laundry Impressions—No. 2.

UP-TO-DATE PLANT IN THE WASH HOUSE

Ours is even more up-to-date—see back

97 'Up-to-date Plant in the Wash House', postcard, 1923.

IMPRESSIONS OF THE DYEING AND DRY CLEANING INDUSTRY

Turnbulls was founded in Hawick in 1819 by John Turnbull as dyers of loose wool yarn and hosiery. Dry cleaning started on a small scale in about 1860, but until 1911 this was a sideline. By the 1920s the domestic dyeing and cleaning side of the business had greatly expanded, and the company also undertook repairs and alterations. They served customers nationwide, relying on the railways to collect and return garments and soft furnishings either directly to clients or through agents. The company seems to have closed in 2002.

Beginning in autumn 1922 they published a quarterly magazine called *Turnbulls Quarterly: A Magazine of Cleaning and Colour* which was sent to customers. In the late 1920s Heath Robinson was employed to make a series of drawings showing his idea of how cleaning and dyeing was done from the earliest time to the present. These were published as double-page spreads in the centre of the magazine (figs 98–102). The subject matter seems to have inspired Heath Robinson to new levels of inventiveness. In the Spring issue of 1931 readers were advised that 'A copy of this picture, suitable for framing, together with previous drawings of the series, can be obtained on application.'

98 'Developing and Testing Dyes', print issued on application, 1931.

SELECTING A DYE FOR A PATCH IN A GENT'S GARMENT.

A TRAINED ARTIST COPYING A TWEED FOR THE REPAIR OF A LAD'S NETHER GARB.

A NEW METHOD OF TESTING THE VIVIDNESS OF THE DYE IN A RED FLANNEL PETTICOAT.

MIXING DYES TO OBTAIN A SKY BLUE FROM NATURE ON THE TILES AT TURNBULLS.

SOME OF THE NEW TESTING CABINETS FOR TESTING FANCY WAISTCOATS DYED BY TURNBULLS LTD. FOR THEIR NON-FADING (TO LIGHT) QUALITIES.

HEATH ROBINSON

Reproduced from 'Turnbulls Quarterly.'

99 'Cleaning Through the Ages', print issued on application, 1931.

100 'Method of Dyeing Children's Clothes in the Stone Ages', print issued on application, 1931.

101 'Dyeing in the Past, Present and Future', print issued on application, 1931.

102 'Up-to-date Methods in a Modern Dye Works', published in *Turnbulls Quarterly*, Autumn 1929.

SOME SECRETS OF THE GENTLEMEN'S OUTFITTING TRADE

Rogers Peet was a New York men's clothing company founded on 6 November 1874. They introduced several innovations into the menswear business: they attached tags to garments giving fabric composition, they marked garments with price tags (the established practice was to haggle), they offered customers their money back if not satisfied, and they used illustrations of specific merchandise in their advertising. The last Rogers Peet store closed in the mid-1980s.

In 1927 Heath Robinson was commissioned to make six drawings and a cover design for this portfolio of loose plates (figs 103–9).

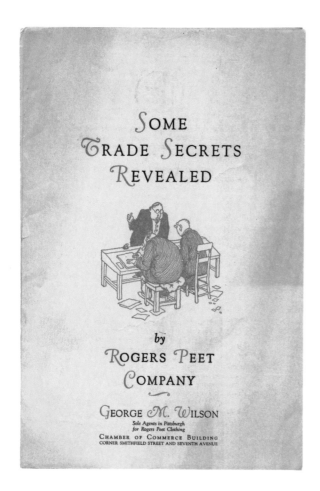

103 The portfolio cover.

104 'Subjecting Cloth to Rogers Peet's Ingenious Sheepdog Test for All Wool', from *Some Trade Secrets Revealed*, 1927.

105 'Clans of MacRogers and MacPeet Rounding-up Mist for Rogers Peet's Scotch Mist Cloth', from *Some Trade Secrets Revealed*, 1927.

106 'A Busy Afternoon in the Weighing Yards of Rogers Peet's Solight Hat Department', from *Some Trade Secrets Revealed*, 1927.

107 'Obtaining Style Reactions at the Monthly Meeting of Rogers Peet Company's Board of Directors', from *Some Trade Secrets Revealed*, 1927.

108 'Up-to-date Tie Tests employed by Messrs. Rogers Peet Company', from *Some Trade Secrets Revealed*, 1927

109 'Research Work by Rogers Peet's Expert Detectives to obtain Data on which to base their Famous 85 Percenter Last for Shoes', from *Some Trade Secrets Revealed*, 1927.

THE MANUFACTURE OF COTTON FABRICS ACCORDING TO HEATH ROBINSON

John Horrocks established a cotton spinning mill in Preston in 1791 and became one of the pioneers of the Lancashire 'factory system'. Horrockses merged with Crewdsen in 1887 to form Horrockses, Crewdson & Co. Ltd. In 1914 their products included 'longcloths, twilled shirtings, cambrics, nainsooks, pillow cottons, plain and twilled sheetings and ready-made sheets, harvards and fancies, and flannelettes'. In 1946 the company launched Horrockses' fashions producing stylish clothing from the company's fabrics.

Heath Robinson's three drawings for this 1922 almanac are amongst his earliest designs to show the manufacturing process (figs 110–12).

110 'Beating and Drawing Out Impurities from Raw Cotton', from *How It Is Done!*, 1921.

111 'Cotton Spinning as
Performed by Spinsters', from
How It Is Done!, 1921.

112 'A Delightfully Ingenious
Method of Weaving with
Patent Scooter Shuttle', from
How It Is Done!, 1921.

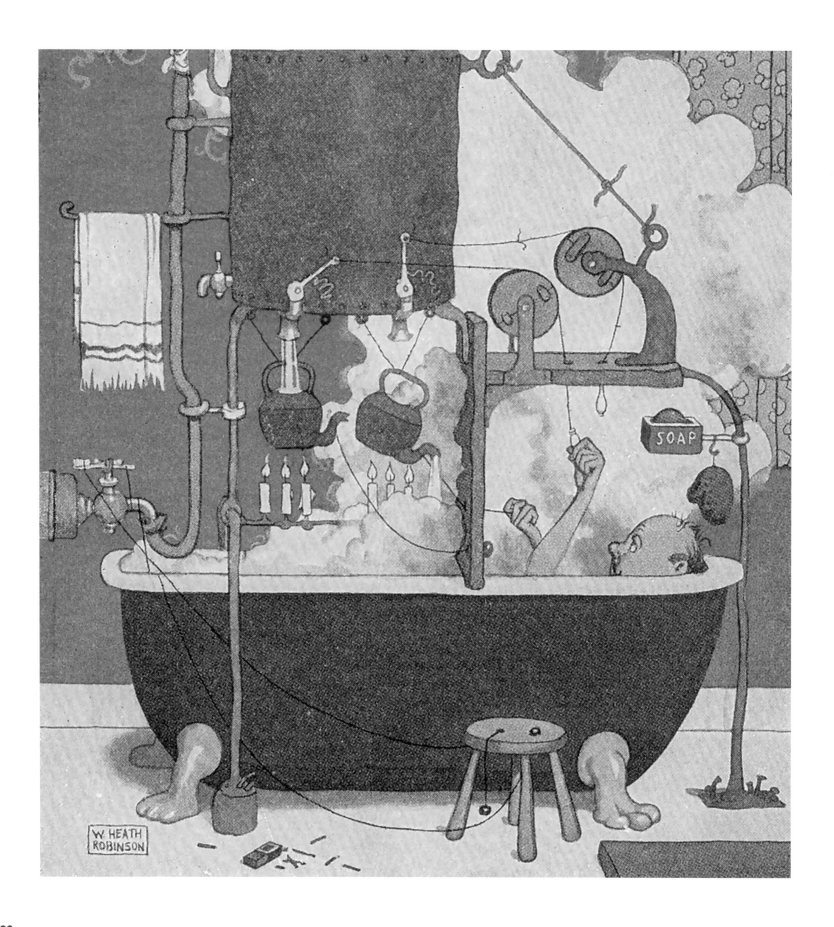

4

AT HOME

Throughout Heath Robinson's career as a humorous artist, domestic life was a frequent subject for his pen. As early as 1911 *The Sketch* magazine published a series of drawings collectively titled 'A Garden Guide', and shortly after the First World War, when subjects other than the war were again being accepted by editors, he made a series of six drawings for *The Bystander* showing 'Spring Cleaning in Full Swing'. However, it was in the 1930s that he became as well known for his domestic scenes as for his contraptions. In 1933 *The Sketch* published a series of six full-page coloured pictures on the theme of 'An Ideal Home'. These included a folding garden for those living on upper floors, space economy at a wedding and a top-floor chicken farm.

The following year he was commissioned by the Ideal Home Exhibition to design his ideal home, 'The Gadgets', which was made by an engineering company, supervised by thc artist. It had more than 30 lifelike moving figures, all busy about their daily tasks.

Two years later, in 1936, Hutchinson published *How to live in a Flat*, the first of a series of four 'How to . . .' books that Heath Robinson wrote with K.R.G.

Browne. It was a masterpiece of gentle humour, satirising the extremes of modernist design in both architecture and furnishings and exploiting to the full the humorous possibilities of vertical living in confined spaces.

Bathrooms and bathing had always offered a ready subject for his humour, especially in each World War, when countering the more extreme press hysteria about how terrifying the enemy was. One of his earliest First World War cartoons had the Kaiser enjoying a morning tub. The subject of one of his first Second World War cartoons was 'Bath Night in the Siegfried Line During an Air Raid'. How better to counter the tales of 'baby-eating Huns' than to show one's enemies naked in the bath? In December 1927 he showed how to avoid embarrassing situations when the bathroom lock is out of order, and in February 1929 he depicted a home-made Turkish bath.

It is not surprising, therefore, that he was called upon to advertise a wide range of products for use in the home and garden. These included henhouses, feather beds, furniture, disinfectant, water heaters, baths and lawnmowers. Perhaps the most

113 Detail of 'With a Clarkhill You Will Have Cheap and Unlimited Hot Water', from *This is a complicated way to obtain hot water, but . . .*, c.1921.

114 'The Interesting Result of a
Visit by the Famous Humorist,
W. Heath Robinson, to Messrs.
Boulton and Paul Limited,
Norwich, the Leading Poultry
Appliance Manufacturers',
published in *Illustrated London
News*, 10 June 1933.

imaginative set of drawings in this chapter are
the 12 showing how one might get the best results
when taking photographs of memorable family
occasions when using Wellington and Ward's roll
films (see figs 129–36). Whether at sporting events,
on the beach, at Christmas lunch, photographing
a new baby or capturing the arrival of the
New Year, gadgets are to the fore in achieving
successful pictures.

FEATHERS AND FEATHER BEDS

The firm of Boulton & Paul, formed in 1905 and
based in Norwich, was a successful general
manufacturing firm. During the First World War
they concentrated on aircraft manufacture and
built more 'Sopwith Camel' fighter planes than
any other company. After the war they provided
most of the structure for the R101 airship. The
aircraft division was sold in 1934 and the company
concentrated on its general manufacturing.
Poultry houses were but a tiny part of the activities
of this major engineering firm. The Norwich
works closed in the 1980s. Heath Robinson's
advertisement for their poultry houses was
published in the *Illustrated London News* in 1933
(fig.114).

Thomas Tapling & Co. Ltd was a furniture
manufacturer and carpet wholesaler based in
London. The company owned a furniture factory
in Finsbury, a bedding factory in East London
and carpet warehouses in Manchester. Heath
Robinson's two drawings for the firm were
reproduced as prints for framing, but they are
undated (fig.115).

116 'Furniture in the Making', published in the *Weekly Herald*, 5 November 1937.

FURNITURE IN THE MAKING

Firth Brothers were manufacturers and retailers of furniture and pianos based in Edmonton and Tottenham in North London. In 1937 one of the brothers, Edward Marmaduke Firth, wrote to Heath Robinson, who lived close by in Highgate, asking him to make some drawings to advertise the company's products. Heath Robinson produced rough sketches of his ideas and invited Mr Firth to visit him at home to discuss them. Many of his proposals met with approval, but a 'Bedside Grand' was replaced by the 'Motor Grand' and the design for players with cold feet was rotated through 90 degrees. A 'Silent Piano' designed not to disturb the neighbours was also discarded. The furniture drawing (fig.116) was published in the local paper in 1937 and the piano drawing (fig.117) the following year. Two of the furniture vignettes were also used in a promotional brochure.

117 'Some Interesting Pianos Not Made by Firth Brothers', published in the *Weekly Herald*, 25 November 1938.

PROBLEMS SOLVED WITH GRE-SOLVENT

The Gre-Solvent Company was based in Leeds and their main product was a paste cleanser sold in round yellow tins. In the 1920s they also sold a 'Gre-Solvent' scouring powder, 'Perco' iron cement and 'Rozinol', a paste soldering flux. The coloured drawing reproduced here (fig.118) was published in 1924 in an advertising booklet called *A Day in the Home of Ease*, edited by the novelist and philanthropist William Pett Ridge. The outlines for the vignettes were reused by the company five years later in a crudely produced booklet titled *The Tale of a Great Discovery* that was printed on rough orange paper at the works. The company is still trading, now based in Wem in Shropshire and producing a wide range of cleaning products aimed at the industrial and institutional markets.

118 'How Dad Inadvertently Brought Home the Gre-Solvent', from *A Day in the Home of Ease*, 1924.

THE MANUFACTURE AND USE OF IZAL DISINFECTANT

Newton, Chambers & Company, Ltd was registered on 24 October 1881 to take over the Thorncliffe ironworks and group of collieries near Sheffield. From the start the company mined its own ironstone and coal. In the late 19th century the firm became interested in the chemistry of coal, and in 1893 discovered Izal, a non-poisonous disinfectant and antiseptic liquid. It was found to be extremely effective, and this along with a vigorous marketing campaign made it the most popular domestic and institutional disinfectant for the next seven decades.

Heath Robinson was recruited to promote Izal in 1924. In his autobiography he describes how he visited the works and 'studied their coke ovens and the methods whereby the valuable by-products are extracted from coal. A ton of coal could be seen taken from the mine at one end of the process and at the other a tube of shaving cream or a bottle of mouthwash. It was miraculous.'[1] His drawings were used to illustrate a 16-page booklet called *Thorncliffe Visited* that was updated and reissued as *How Izal is Made* (figs 119–23). There was also a series of ten postcards and a number of vignettes from the drawings were printed in green on Izal toilet paper.

119 'A Busy Corner at Thorncliffe Showing the Pits from which the Coal is Extracted. Selecting and washing and preparing it for distillation', from *Thorncliffe Visited*, 1924.

120 'Coal Cooking. Converting Coal into Coke and Gas', from *Thorncliffe Visited*, 1924.

121 'Condensing Crude Oil from this Special Gas and Izal Oil from the Crude Oil', from *Thorncliffe Visited*, 1924.

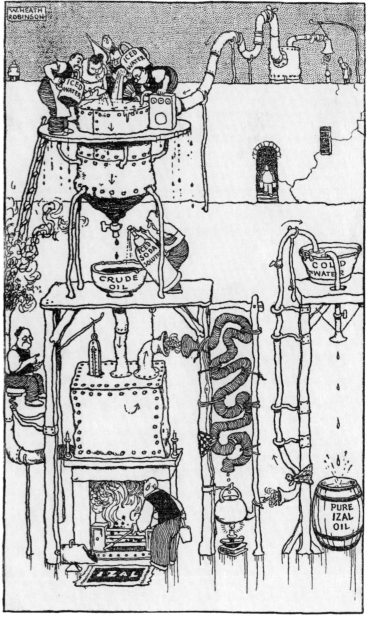

THE AFTERGLOW OF AN IZAL BATH

122 'The Afterglow of an Izal Bath', from *Thorncliffe Visited*, 1924.

123 'Izal in Malarial Swamps', from *Thorncliffe Visited*, 1924.

IZAL IN MALARIAL SWAMPS.

124 'Different Methods of Overcoming Bathroom Difficulties!', published in *Town and Country Homes*, February 1929.

METHODS OF OVERCOMING
BATHROOM DIFFICULTIES

The 'Veronic' bath was made by Rownson, Drew & Clydesdale Ltd, a light engineering firm based at Upper Thames Street in London. The company had been founded in 1821 and specialised in making elevators, conveyors and mechanical handling equipment. In 1909 they manufactured the 'Donald' elevator, which was used to carry bananas to and from ships' holds. By the 1920s, Rowsons had diversified into package handling, warehousing and hardware.

Their porcelain-enamelled baths were available in 1929 from £8.5s.0d complete with front panel and mixer fittings. The drawing shown here was published in *Town and Country Homes*, February 1929 (fig.124). Particulars of their range, with a copy of Heath Robinson's drawing, could be obtained by sending a postcard to the company.

HOT WATER THE
HEATH ROBINSON WAY

Clarkhills Automatic Water Heaters Ltd had their works in Vauxhall Bridge Road in London. They made gas-powered water heaters and specialised in hot water systems that provided instant hot water to any part of a house. They held a patent for a special distribution valve.

Heath Robinson's design for the company dates from about 1926 and it was reproduced in an article on 'Humour in Advertising' in *Commercial Art* magazine in 1927 (fig.125). The author was unable to categorise Heath Robinson's work, merely commenting that: 'Probably the most unique style of humorous drawing available today is that of Heath Robinson. The quaint absurdity of his amazing mechanical contrivances and the comic seriousness of his characters are a never-failing source of delight.'[2] The advertising agents for the project were Travers, Cleaver, Ltd.

125 An Advertising Brochure for Clarkhill Water Heaters, c.1921.

ALL "CLARKHILL" HEATERS
ARE OF BRITISH MANUFACTURE

This is a complicated way to obtain hot water but . . . .

With a "Clarkhill"
you will have
Cheap and Unlimited Hot Water
throughout the house at a moment's notice

HEATH ROBINSON'S IMPRESSIONS OF RANSOMES' MOTOR MOWERS

Ransomes, Sims & Jefferies was a major British agricultural machinery maker producing a wide range of products including traction engines, trolleybuses, ploughs, lawnmowers, combine harvesters and other tilling equipment. They were based in Ipswich. Founded in 1879, the company is still in business.

They employed Heath Robinson to advertise their motor mowers in 1928, and his drawings were used in coloured and black-and-white versions, as full-page or half-page advertisements (figs 126–8). Versions exist with the captions in English, German and Dutch. They paid 35 guineas for the full-page drawing in black and white and a further £6 to have it coloured at a later date.

126 (below top) 'The Housewife', from a manufacturer's proof.

127 (BELOW BOTTOM) 'W. Heath Robinson's Impressions of Ransomes' Motor Mowers', published in *The Sketch*, 3 April 1929.

"THE HOUSEWIFE"
ONE OF THE LATEST TYPES OF MOTOR LAWN MOWERS FOR ENABLING THE HOUSEWIFE TO CARRY ON WHILE MOWING THE LAWN

W. HEATH ROBINSON'S IMPRESSIONS OF RANSOMES' MOTOR MOWERS

A HANDY MUSICAL MOTOR MOWER FOR KEEPING IN DANCING PRACTICE DURING THE SUMMER MONTHS WITHOUT NEGLECTING THE LAWN

"MOTHER'S DELIGHT"

A NEW MOTOR MOWER SPECIALLY DESIGNED TO ENABLE MOTHER TO CARRY ON WITH HER DOMESTIC DUTIES WHEN MOWING THE LAWN

W. HEATH ROBINSON

SAVING TROUBLE IN THE HOME

The specialist lithographic printing company Thomas Forman and Sons of Nottingham had first worked with Heath Robinson in 1907 when they printed 40 coloured plates by him for *The Monarchs of Merry England,* a comic history in verse by Roland Carse. In 1931 they decided commission a set of six humorous drawings to be used in bespoke calendars for small businesses. These were published under the title 'Brain Waves' (figs 172–78). They must have proved popular since the following year a second set were commissioned under the title 'To Save Trouble', (changed to 'Saving Trouble' in the published version). The example of the second calendar seen has no business imprint, so must have been sold directly to the public.

128 (ABOVE LEFT). 'A new machine for drawing a cork without strain', from the 'Saving Trouble' calendar, 1934.

(ABOVE RIGHT). 'The Lullaby Bed. To save getting out of bed to rock the baby when he is troublesome at night', from the 'Saving Trouble' calendar, 1934.

129 'Wedding Group Photography: Some simple suggestions for photographing the party without unduly embarrassing the Bride and Bridegroom', from *The Light Side of Photography*, 1925.

130 'Photography on the Cricket Field: How instructive snaps may be taken of the actual play on the cricket field', from *The Light Side of Photography*, 1925.

THE LIGHT SIDE OF PHOTOGRAPHY

Wellington & Ward was a company founded by the English photographer and scientist John Wellington. He had collaborated with George Eastman, founder of the Eastman Kodak company (later shortened to Kodak) and inventor of roll film, in America in the 1880s. Wellington's firm became Wellington & Ward in 1911. By 1930 it had merged with Ilford.

Heath Robinson was fascinated by both the technical and social aspects of photography. As early as 1914 he had first satirised photography in a brilliantly conceived series of four pictures on 'Press Photographing' in which cartoons on the subject of discreet photography were drawn with distortions that suggest the disasters that might result from one's first experiments with a box camera. A number of his subsequent cartoons feature devices for self-photography or for snapping animals in the wild. Here, perhaps, is the origin of the 'selfie'. These ideas are developed in a promotional booklet for Wellington & Ward, which was published in 1925 (figs 129–36).

131 'Seaside Photography: How to secure charming and unaffected photographs on the beach', from *The Light Side of Photography*, 1925.

132 'More Seaside Photography: A simple method of securing pleasing snapshots of channel swimmers and others', from *The Light Side of Photography*, 1925.

133 'Animal Photography: Some simple devices for securing interesting snaps of animal life with rustic backgrounds', from *The Light Side of Photography*, 1925.

134 'On the River: The simplest and surest methods of securing happy snapshots of river scenes', from *The Light Side of Photography*, 1925.

135 (OPPOSITE) 'Big Game Photography: How to snap big game in its native haunts', from *The Light Side of Photography*, 1925.

136 'Hints for Christmas: How to take a flashlight of the Xmas Dinner Party', from *The Light Side of Photography*, 1925.

STRUCTURAL ALTERATIONS

REMOVING A HOUSE IN THE DEAD OF NIGHT
FROM THE NEIGHBOURHOOD OF A DUSTBIN

Drawn by W. Heath Robinson.

A POPULAR IMPRESSION OF
THE BOVIS BOARD ROOM

Drawn by W. Heath Robinson.

PROPERTY MANAGEMENT BY BOVIS LTD

Heath Robinson contributed two images in 1919 to
a portfolio of designs issued by Bovis Ltd to advertise
their services as contractors and decorators
(figs 137–8). Other artists represented include
Lawson Wood, H.M. Batcman, George Morrow,
Herbert Samuel ('Bert') Thomas and Alfred Leete.

137 'Structural alterations',
from 'Bovisms' portfolio, 1919.

138 'A Popular Impression of
the Bovis Board Room', from
'Bovisms' portfolio, 1919.

W. HEATH ROBINSON

5

RADIO

It was Heath Robinson's increasing celebrity as a humorist that led him into the world of broadcasting. He had been a regular contributor to *The Bystander* since 1905, when one of his earliest cartoons had appeared in its pages, and in April 1923 an unusual competition run by that magazine introduced him to radio broadcasting. The competition was called 'Drawings by Wireless'. Heath Robinson, speaking from the studio at London's radio station 2LO, described to listeners a drawing he had made of the difficulties of erecting an aerial. Those wishing to participate in the competition were then invited to make a sketch in the style of Mr Heath Robinson and to send it to *The Bystander*. The winning entry would be the one that came closest to the original drawing that had been described. A prize of ten guineas was offered and the best drawings were published in a subsequent issue of the magazine. The winning entry looks more like the artist's published work than the simple sketch that he had prepared for the broadcast!

The following year Heath Robinson made a series of drawings for an advertising booklet published by Philips Glowlamp Works Ltd picturing *The Wireless*

Adventures of Mr. Pimple (figs 139–45). In this he demonstrates how a choice of inferior valves leads to dejection, while happiness results from the wise purchase of the advertised brand. Similar themes were adopted later to advertise Osram valves (figs 149–50). Contentment results from a well-functioning radio, no matter how squalid one's surroundings. Even a soap advertisement shows radio to be an essential ingredient of comfort (fig.146).

Heath Robinson's only venture into animated films occurred in the mid-1920s when he was persuaded to make a short cartoon advertising Amplion loudspeakers, which styled themselves as 'The World's Standard Wireless Loud-Speaker'. The film was called *The Tale of the Amplion*. It demonstrates his ability to adapt his style to the medium and subject he was working on. It also shows his inclination towards the surreal when circumstances (and editors) permitted. In it, speakers transform into an old woman, a goose laying eggs and a lion who eats the old woman. There can be little doubt that the time taken to make the large number of drawings required for even a short film and the relatively meagre rewards would have

139 Detail from 'Mr. Pimple now buys Phillips' Receiving Valves . . .', from *The Wireless Adventures of Mr. Pimple*, 1924.

discouraged both Heath Robinson and his agent from returning to the medium.

In late 1940, in common with many other businesses in London, Webb's Radio, of 14 Soho Street, W1, lost their showroom windows in a bombing raid. Normal practice was to replace the glass windows with wooden panelling. Webb's decided to make a virtue of this and commissioned Heath Robinson to make a design for the new windows to show that 'Webb's Radio Carry on and Deliver the Goods' (figs 147–8). The design was produced and the artist Norman Keene was employed to transfer it to the wooden substitute windows. A large print of the design was made and sent to customers.

Mr. Pimple's dream of happiness.

Mr. Pimple studies up the subject with a view to making a wireless set for the family.

140 'Mr. Pimple's dream of happiness', from *The Wireless Adventures of Mr. Pimple*, 1924.

Mr. Pimple begins with the aerial — not forgetting a coat of paint.

Mr. Pimple is ingenious and finds a use for everything.

Taking the lead in (magnetic method).

Nothing comes amiss.

141 'Mr. Pimple begins with the aerial . . .', from *The Wireless Adventures of Mr. Pimple*, 1924.

142 'Taking the lead in (magnetic method)', from *The Wireless Adventures of Mr. Pimple*, 1924.

THE WIRELESS ADVENTURES OF MR PIMPLE

Philips Glowlamp Works Ltd, located at Eindhoven in Holland, was established as a limited company in 1912 for the manufacture of incandescent light bulbs. By 1924 it was employing 6,000 workers and was making thermionic valves as well as light bulbs. The firm had extensive research facilities and was a model employer, providing accommodation for its workers. The management paid careful attention to everything concerning the lives of their people.

Heath Robinson's booklet tells the story of Mr Pimple's wireless adventures in six major and six minor drawings (figs 140–45). These progress from Mr Pimple's dream of happiness, through erection of the aerial, taking in the lead, burying the earth, finding that the completed radio yielded no sound, presentation by a friend of a Philips valve and final success. The illustrations, in the style of his children's book *Peter Quip in Search of a Friend*, are delightfully drawn, particularly the family dancing to music from the radio, making this one of the most attractive of his advertising booklets.

As well as being issued in Britain and the Commonwealth, it was published in Holland with a Dutch text.

Mr. Pimple now carefully earths the earth wire.

At last everything is ready, but alas, no result is obtained.

Mr. Pimple is in despair.

143 'Mr. Pimple now carefully earths the earth wire', from *The Wireless Adventures of Mr. Pimple*, 1924.

144 'At last everything is ready, but alas, no result is obtained', from *The Wireless Adventures of Mr. Pimple*, 1924.

Mr. Pimple now buys Philips' Receiving Valves every time and discovers that they give the very best results.

145 'Mr. Pimple now buys Phillips' Receiving Valves every time and discovers that they give the very best results', from *The Wireless Adventures of Mr. Pimple*, 1924.

HEATH ROBINSON'S IDEA OF COMFORT

Radio clearly played an important part in Heath
Robinson's idea of comfort, as can be seen in his
advertisement for 'Comfort' soap published in
1924 (fig.146). It was one of a series of 12 drawings
in which different artists each depicted their idea
of comfort.

146 'Heath Robinson's Idea
of Comfort', published in *The
Humorist*, 10 May 1924.

147 'Webb's Radio Carry On and Deliver the Goods', 1940, halftone print, 220 × 560 mm (8⅝ × 22 in).

148 Webb's Radio's wooden window, 10 January 1941. (Hulton Picture Library, reproduced by permission of Getty Images)

WEBB'S RADIO CARRY ON AND DELIVER THE GOODS

Webb's Radio commissioned Heath Robinson to produce a design for the wooden windows that replaced glass shattered at their premises in the Blitz in late 1940 (fig.147). A large print of the design was sent to customers with an accompanying note saying that: 'The Heath Robinson Cartoon which we are sending you with our compliments depicts in a typical manner the attitude of the Britisher to Germany's Blitzkreig [*sic*].'

A photograph taken on 10 January 1941, preserved in the Hulton Archive, shows the new windows in place (fig.148).

FINE TUNING

The Marconi-Osram Valve Company was a British manufacturer of thermionic valves. A subsidiary of the (British) General Electric Company Ltd, it was founded in 1919, when the valve-making interests of GEC (Osram) and the Marconi Company were combined. In 1929, Marconi sold its interest in the company to the Gramophone Company, a predecessor of EMI.

Heath Robinson made two drawings for the company in 1934 (figs 149–50). It is not known which newspaper these cuttings were clipped from.

Give your set a tonic with OSRAM VALVES! It is perfectly natural for the best of valves to drop in efficiency after long use. The symptoms are — drop in power, drop in purity and fewer stations.

149 'Give your set a tonic with Osram Valves – I', c.1934, unidentified newspaper cutting.

WRITE for a copy of the OSRAM WIRELESS GUIDE (1932 Edition) which gives full particulars of the complete range of OSRAM VALVES as well as tables of recommended types for all well-known

Make up your mind to have better radio this Winter. Give your set a tonic with OSRAM VALVES. This is a prescription that immediately will enable your set to give more power, better purity, and many more stations.

150 'Give your set a tonic with Osram Valves – II', c.1934, unidentified newspaper cutting.

6

PAPER AND PRINTING

Not surprisingly, Heath Robinson was in demand to advertise the products of papermakers and companies that supported the printing industry. Amongst the papermakers that called on his services were Thomas & Green of Soho Mills, Wooburn Green, Buckinghamshire, who opted for a single large coloured illustration of 'The Art of Paper Making as Explained by W. Heath Robinson' (fig.162). Vickery's focused on their research and advanced papermaking technology in a series of line drawings (figs 158–60). Both companies issued the advertisements printed on samples of their papers. The German papermakers Zerkall Bütten also chose the papermaking process as the subject of their advertisements, but with a surreal twist, suggesting that live goats were used in the making of their animal size (figs 155–7).

Shuck, Maclean & Co. were makers of fine printing inks, and in their advertising their aim was to show off the qualities of those inks. To this end they commissioned a number of portfolios of humorous drawings by well-known artists. Each contained six drawings with a common theme. Heath Robinson contributed to at least three collections (figs 151–4).

The themes were 'Life without Printing Ink', 'Testimonials and Otherwise' and 'Printing Ink in the Home', and each gave him ample scope for his inventiveness. Particularly satisfying is the scene of printers attempting to find alternatives to printing ink while their press stands idle.

Another ancillary trade was that of plate making. Founded in 1921, the Practical Etching Service specialised in high-quality process engraving. In 1931 they commissioned Heath Robinson to make a series of halftone illustrations of the various stages of the plate-making process (figs 165–71), together with a large coloured illustration to show off their skills in colour reproduction (fig.164), and a cover design for a 28-page promotional booklet called *The Gentle Art of Reproducing* (fig.163). The cover design is bizarre in the extreme, illustrating the art of reproducing with a turkey hatching a large number of eggs, from each of which comes a reproduction of the cover design.

Heath Robinson's reputation was such that printers or publishers would use it to attract advertisers. In 1923 the *Evening News* invited him to design a page of advertisements with a pictorial banner heading 'Inventions by W. Heath Robinson'

151 Detail from 'Laudable but Pathetic Efforts on the Part of Printers to Carry on without Ink', from *Life Without Printing Ink*, undated (1920s).

and incorporating his photograph (fig.180). Eight of the nine panels below this were then sold to different companies for whom he drew an individual advertisement. The ninth panel announced a children's painting competition with cash prizes for the best colouring of the W. Heath Robinson drawings on the page.

Thomas Forman & Sons, the Nottingham lithographic printers, commissioned 12 coloured pictures of Heath Robinson's contraptions (figs 172–78). These were incorporated in calendars for small businesses that otherwise would never be able to afford such work. These finely produced calendars must have greatly impressed the favoured customers who received them.

THE SHUCK MACLEAN PORTFOLIOS

Shuck Maclean were printing ink manufacturers with premises in Gunpowder Alley, off Shoe Lane, just north of London's Fleet Street. They were established in 1914 and continued trading until the 1960s. In 1919 they commissioned six artists to make one coloured picture each on the subject of 'Testimonials and Otherwise', and these were issued as a portfolio to potential customers to demonstrate the excellence of their inks (fig.152).

The venture must have been successful as two similar portfolios followed in the next few years, each with a contribution from Heath Robinson. Their subjects were 'Life Without Printing Ink' (fig.153) and 'Printing Ink in the Home' (fig.154).

153 'Laudable but Pathetic Efforts on the Part of Printers to Carry on without Ink', from *Life Without Printing Ink*, undated (1920s).

154 'Thousands of Other Useful Purposes are Served by the Use of Printing Ink in the Home, a few of which are suggested here', from *Printing Ink in the Home*, c.1930.

155 'Zerkall Bütten auf der machine geshöpft' [Zerkall mould made, drawn from the machine], undated postcard.

156 'an der luft getrocknet' [air-dried], undated postcard.

157 'tierisch geleimt' [animal-sized], undated postcard.

PAPER MAKING THE GERMAN WAY

Zerkall is a village in North Rhine-Westphalia known for its paper mill. Paper has been made there since the end of the 19th century, and since 1920 the main product has been hand-made paper marketed under the registered trademark 'ZERKALL MOULD MADE'. The mill is a major employer in the region and is still run by the Renker family.

There is no firm evidence as to the date at which Heath Robinson designed advertisements for the company, but on stylistic grounds it appears to have been around 1924.

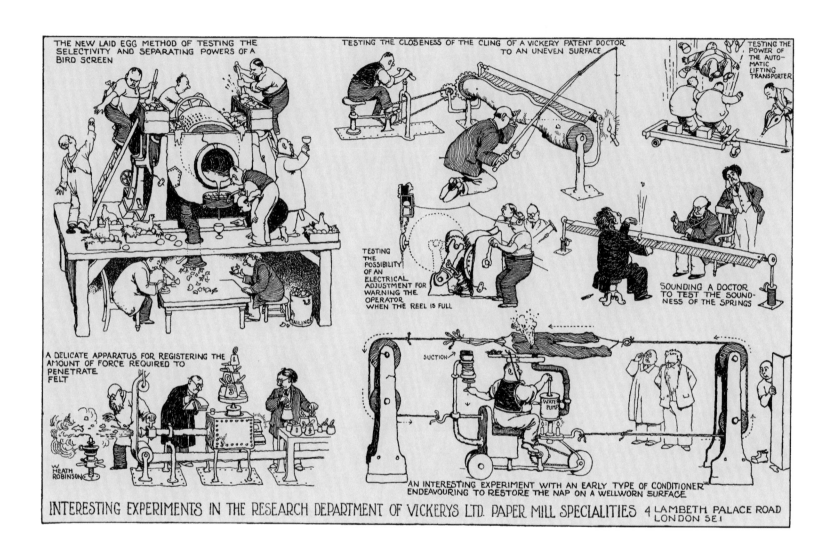

The illustration contains the following labels:

THE NEW LAID EGG METHOD OF TESTING THE SELECTIVITY AND SEPARATING POWERS OF A BIRD SCREEN

TESTING THE CLOSENESS OF THE CLING OF A VICKERY PATENT DOCTOR TO AN UNEVEN SURFACE

TESTING THE POWER OF THE AUTOMATIC LIFTING TRANSPORTER

TESTING THE POSSIBILITY OF AN ELECTRICAL ADJUSTMENT FOR WARNING THE OPERATOR WHEN THE REEL IS FULL

SOUNDING A DOCTOR TO TEST THE SOUNDNESS OF THE SPRINGS

A DELICATE APPARATUS FOR REGISTERING THE AMOUNT OF FORCE REQUIRED TO PENETRATE FELT

HEATH ROBINSON

SUCTION

WATER PUMP

AN INTERESTING EXPERIMENT WITH AN EARLY TYPE OF CONDITIONER ENDEAVOURING TO RESTORE THE NAP ON A WELLWORN SURFACE

INTERESTING EXPERIMENTS IN THE RESEARCH DEPARTMENT OF VICKERYS LTD. PAPER MILL SPECIALITIES 4 LAMBETH PALACE ROAD LONDON SE1

VICKERY'S ADVANCED PAPERMAKING METHODS

Vickery's, established some time before 1914 as Vickery's Patents Ltd, printers' engineers, were makers of machinery for papermaking. In particular, they held a patent for the 'doctor', a device for removing excess water and fibres from the rollers in papermaking machinery, which was invented by Dr Frederick Vickery in 1909.

Heath Robinson's drawings for Vickery's were made during the late 1920s or early 1930s to be used in trade journals and to be printed on samples of their paper for use at trade shows (figs 158–60). They refer to both the 'doctor' and the 'bird screen', a rotary screen used in papermaking invented by the American Charles Sumner Bird. The drawing of *Stages in the Evolution of Vickery Doctoring* was reprinted in the trade journal *Paper* in 1979 to celebrate the centenary of that publication.

158 'Interesting Experiments in the Research Department of Vickerys Ltd. Paper Mill Specialities', late 1920s/early 1930s, print on heavy card.

159 'Stages in the Evolution of Vickery Doctoring', late 1920s/early 1930s, print on heavy card.

160 'The Triple Treatment Research Department in Full Swing', illustration from a display card for Vickery's, late 1920s/early 1930s. A caption beneath the illustration reads: 'Purifuging is the Centrifugalisation of paper stock by Triple Treatment. By this system, a remarkable standard of purification can be attained as the stock is submitted to three different and distinct treatments, each under a different condition of centrifugal action and travel.'

AN INSTRUCTIVE AFTERNOON AT THE KADO CARBON PAPER WORKS

Kado Ltd were located at 35 Ely Place in the London district of Clerkenwell, close to the City. They manufactured carbon paper and typewriter ribbons.

The Heath Robinson drawing shown here was printed on the back of a guide to which carbon paper to use for various purposes (fig.161). It was also reproduced in the *Official Guide to Holborn* in 1937.

161 An advertising drawing for Kado carbon paper, published in *The Official Guide to Holborn*, fifth edition, 1937.

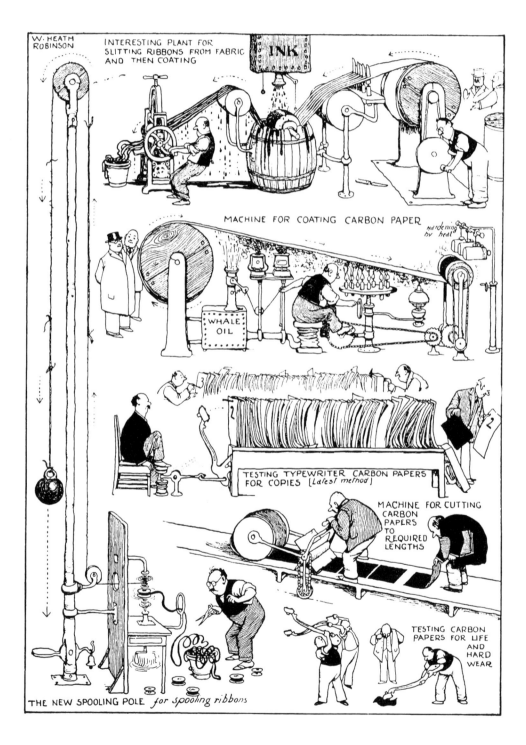

THE ART OF PAPERMAKING EXPLAINED

The partnership of John Thomas, Edwin Thomas and Roland Green was formed in 1881, although paper had been made at Soho Mills in Wooburn, Buckinghamshire, for a long time before that. John Thomas was knighted in 1907. The company was still at Soho Mills in 1952 when a pension scheme for staff was established, but has since specialised in paper products for the food and medical industries and moved to Peterborough.

In 1921 Heath Robinson made a design for a wall calendar for the papermakers Thomas & Green (fig.162). The finished watercolour was delivered to A.E. Johnson who then had the lettering put in. The rectangle at the bottom, centre, would have had a block of daily calendar tear-off pages. The image was also used as an advertising insert in printing trade journals, printed on a sample of their paper. The company had a series of glass slides made of the individual vignettes in the drawing for use at lectures.

In 1922 they commissioned a further design, a large line drawing of the papermaking process in action, for use in press advertisements. That image is unusual in having a large degree of slapstick in it.

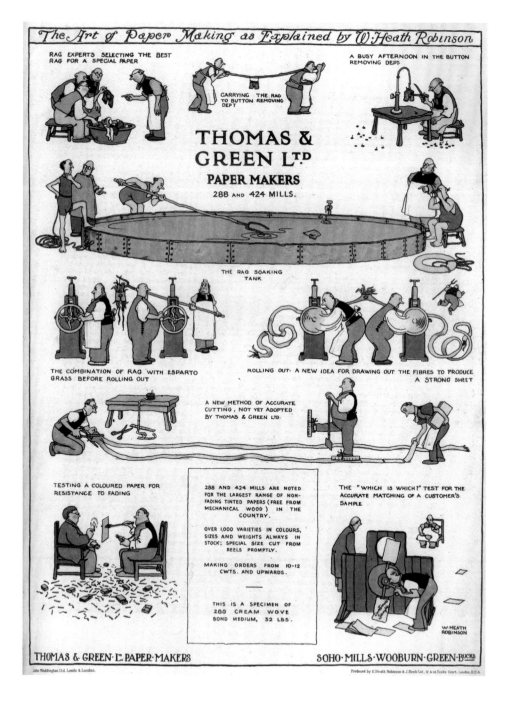

162 'The Art of Paper Making as Explained by W. Heath Robinson', calendar, 1921.

THE GENTLE ART OF REPRODUCING

The Practical Etching Service Ltd was
incorporated in September 1921 and had
premises at 53–55 Great Sutton Street in London's
Clerkenwell district where they remained until
the Second World War. The company provided
the services of artists, designers, photographers
and process engravers for publishers and
advertisers. Heath Robinson's booklet promoting
the company was published in 1931 (figs 163–71).
The foreword concludes with the statement that
'in coming to us for blocks of any kind you can
be sure of the utmost efficiency for high quality
work and service'. The halftone illustrations
manage to remain true to the essential nature of
the plate-making process while incorporating
Heath Robinson's unique view of how it might be
accomplished.

163 *The Gentle Art of*
Reproducing, 1931, cover.

164 A double-page coloured picture that folds out from the back of the booklet *The Gentle Art of Reproducing*. It has no caption, but indicates the range of clients that were served by the company.

165 'Committee of Trained Experts Deciding on Best Method to Pursue with Each Drawing', from *The Gentle Art of Reproducing*, 1931.

166 'The New Patent Air Brush in use in the Studio – preparing a drawing for reproduction', from *The Gentle Art of Reproducing*, 1931.

COMMITTEE OF TRAINED EXPERTS DECIDING ON BEST METHOD TO PURSUE WITH EACH DRAWING

W HEATH ROBINSON

THE NEW PATENT AIR BRUSH IN USE IN THE STUDIO *preparing a drawing for reproduction*

W. HEATH ROBINSON

167 'Coating the Plate with a Carefully Mixed Solution of Fish Glue, White of Egg &c. &c.', from *The Gentle Art of Reproducing*, 1931.

168 'Washing and Drying Negatives after Developing and Fixing for Line, Halftone or Colour Reproduction', from *The Gentle Art of Reproducing*, 1931.

MOUNTING PLATES
ON WOOD FOR BLACK
AND WHITE AND
COLOUR PRINTING

TAKING A PROOF

THE ETCHING BATH
A new method of etching plates

KEEP CUSTOMERS HAPPY WITH HEATH ROBINSON'S 'BRAIN WAVES'

In 1848 Thomas Forman acquired the business of Printer and Stationer on Long Row, Nottingham. In 1870 new premises were built in Sherwood Street, and the company became Thos. Forman & Sons. Colour printing, general printing and the publication of newspapers were continued side by side until 1919, when they ceased printing newspapers. In 1926 they built a new 5-acre factory equipped with the latest machinery, and in 1927 they announced that the company 'is in close collaboration with the most successful artists of the day and has at all times a large selection of pictures suitable as advertisements for different trades. Their reproduction is in the hands of the most capable artists procurable, by the latest methods and the newest processes.'[1] They had already used some of the illustrations from Heath Robinson's book *The Monarchs of Merry England* (1904) to produce advertising postcards for small traders. In 1931 they commissioned six coloured illustrations on the theme of 'Inventions' to be used in tailor-made calendars for small businesses (fig.172). Heath Robinson received £180 for the copyright in these images (fig.173) which were published under the title 'Brain Waves' (figs 174–78). A further six drawings under the title 'To Save Trouble' were commissioned the following year on the same terms. The lithographic printing process used means that these are amongst the finest examples of Heath Robinson's humorous works in colour.

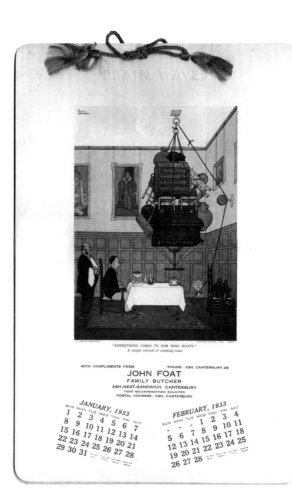

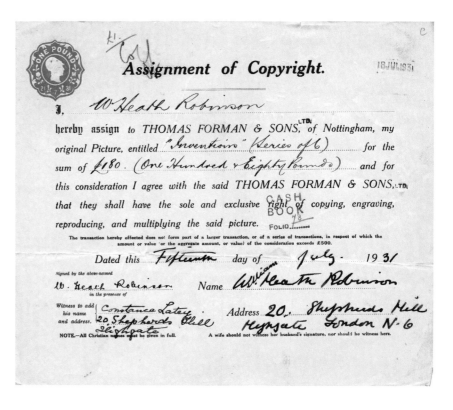

172 A calendar made for John Foat, a family butcher in Ash-next-Sandwich, Canterbury, 1933.

173 Copyright certificate signed by Heath Robinson assigning rights to Thomas Forman & Sons.

174 '"Two's Company, Three's None", Sensible Precaution against Sudden Interruption of Confidential Conversation', from the 1933 'Brain Waves' series calendar.

W. HEATH ROBINSON

FORMAN. NOTTM. ENG.　1805

175 '"It Takes Two to Make a Quarrel", how to smooth over those little differences that sometimes occur in Bridge', from the 1933 'Brain Waves' series calendar.

176 '"Early to Bed and Early to Rise" etc., etc., an ingenious device for getting up in good time in the morning', from the 1933 'Brain Waves' series calendar.

W. HEATH ROBINSON.

FORMAN NOTTM ENG. 1805

177 '"All is fair in Love and War". A cleverly planned elopement', from the 1933 'Brain Waves' series calendar.

178 '"Fire is a Good Servant but a Bad Master". An elegant apparatus for lighting a cigar in safety', from the 'Brain Waves' series calendar.

W. HEATH ROBINSON

FORMAN, NOTTM., ENG. 1805

179 Page 16 of the *Evening Standard*, 1 January 1934.

INNOVATIONS IN NEWSPRINT

The page of advertisements published in the *Evening News* on 27 July 1923 was the first of a number of similar commissions (fig.180). The idea was picked up by the rival *Evening Standard* in a series of New Year advertising supplements that featured in the first issue of the year in most years between 1932 and 1940 (fig.179). In total there were seven such supplements, of which Heath Robinson supplied the drawings for four (Bert Thomas, Gilbert Wilkinson and 'Ridgewell' (William Leigh Ridgewell) undertaking one each). The supplements occupied one or two pages of the paper and consisted of a pictorial title-piece over quarter-page line drawings advertising various products. The same products often appear from year to year, the most regular being Nugget boot polish, Smith's Sectric clocks and Wright's coal tar soap.

180 Page 8 of *The Evening News*, 27 July 1923.

7

SEA, AIR AND RAIL TRANSPORT

In 1930 Heath Robinson was one of the artists invited to contribute to the decoration of the *Empress of Britain*, a new luxury liner being built on the Clyde for the Canadian Pacific Railway Company (CPR). Writing about this project, the editor of *The Studio* said in 1931: 'In constructing the latest and biggest addition to their fleet the CPR have succeeded in presenting to the world an exhibition of the concerted efforts of British talent and British manufacture. Seldom, in recent times, can one point to a more successful example of what Britain stands for in fine quality of material linked with superb craftsmanship and engineering.'[1] Heath Robinson was responsible for the decoration of the children's room and the cocktail bar, and his designs were painted on large wooden panels in his studio (figs 9 and 186–7). Sadly, the ship was requisitioned as a troop transport in 1939 and was sunk by enemy action on 26th October 1940. All that remains of Heath Robinson's designs are two small trial panels, two watercolours and some advertising booklets (figs 182–5).

In 1935, the Great Western Railway celebrated its centenary by commissioning Heath Robinson to make a collection of drawings depicting the past, present and future of the company (figs 188–94). The book had 96 pages with 45 full-page line drawings and a similar number of smaller drawings. It was published in card wrappers priced at one shilling. There was also a special edition in hard covers for presentation to shareholders.

An earlier commission relating to logistic infrastructure came in 1921, when Heath Robinson was asked to illustrate a substantial production by the Port of Manchester Warehouses (figs 195–200). This was called *Then and Now* and was designed to promote the use of Manchester as a port by demonstrating its sophisticated modern handling and storage facilities, and to encourage companies to locate their factories on the adjacent Trafford Park Estate to take full advantage of those facilities. Heath Robinson's drawings showed his view of 'Then', whilst the 'Now' was illustrated with photographs. The first of the six full-page drawings in the book shows the 'supposed origin of the warehouse – an early effort to preserve a filbert through the winter months' and features a group of Stone Age men building the warehouse from rocks and animal skins.

181 Detail from 'Mr W. Heath Robinson's Own Private Railway Engine, not often allowed onto the G.W.R.' .

Particularly convincing are the drawings featuring bales of cotton, showing their 'infinite capacity for repose'.

Heath Robinson's last advertising commission came in 1941 when he was invited to make a series of pen-and-wash illustrations of Royal Air Force jargon under the general heading 'The War in the Air' for High Duty Alloys of Slough (figs 10 and 202–9). At the time he was making a weekly drawing for *The Sketch*, and these drawings, which were published in *Flight* and *The Aeroplane,* are in a similar vein. Copies of the earlier drawings in the series could be obtained by writing to the company, but this offer was discontinued part way through the series, presumably because of the wartime paper shortage.

THE EMPRESS OF BRITAIN – THE KNICKERBOCKER BAR

The designs for the walls of the cocktail bar on the *Empress of Britain* showed the story of cocktails (figs 182–7). There were also a number of circular trompe-l'oeil panels in the ceiling showing faces looking down, a parachutist dropping in, or a ramshackle aeroplane passing overhead. The decorations were the basis of an article by Anthony Armstrong called 'The Story of Cocktails' which was published in *The Strand Magazine* in December 1931 and was reprinted by CPR as an advertising brochure. In 1938 the same set of illustrations were used in *Cocktail Mixing*, a small, 12-page booklet containing a number of cocktail recipes.

182 An original design for the *Empress of Britain* cocktail bar, 1930/31, watercolour, 270 × 375 mm (10⅝ × 14¾ in).

183 'Grading and Picking Cherries; Stoning Cherries; Polishing Cherries; Putting the Sticks into Cherries", from *The Story of Cocktails*, 1932.

THE COCKTAIL BIRD

Gently, Sir. Gently with that bird! That's the Cocktail Bird. And *that*, Madam, is the famous Heath Robinson Cocktail Cherry. Wonderful things, cocktail cherries . . . but they never did receive their proper dignity (if I may say so, Madam) until Mr. Heath Robinson put them on the map (if I may be excused the pun, Sir) by sending their story round the world on the famous Empress of Britain cocktail panels. Yes, Canadian Pacific Ship, Sir, that's right . . . and you soon spot the panels in her Knickerbocker Bar as being the real Heath Robinson recipe. (You'd prefer a Martini ?) Yes, I agree, Sir. It takes a Heath Robinson to use bits of string and

wire in a cocktail shake-up with any success. But actually, I understand he does a lot of serious work too . . . very delightful book illustrations . . . in Kipling's " Song of the English," for example. Very unassuming fellow . . . one of three brother artists. Bet he enjoyed that Empress of Britain job one of the best he's done. Who wouldn't . . . for a ship like that ? Oh, no, Sir, actually the panels were done in his London Studio . . . and the wood alone is a rare bit of stuff, I believe. You should see them yourself sometime. A trip in the Empress of Britain sort of lifts the crème de la crème off the Ocean, Sir. Thank you, Sir. Good night, Madam.

COCKTAIL COURAGE

GRADING AND PICKING CHERRIES

STONING CHERRIES

POLISHING CHERRIES

PUTTING THE STICKS   INTO CHERRIES

A PLEASANT SURPRISE

IN THE CLOUDS

THE COCKTAIL IN THE FAR EAST

SKY HIGH

CLARIFYING COCKTAILS

NAMING NEW COCKTAILS

In *The Story of Cocktails*, the editor writes:

> Apart altogether from the fact that his entertaining designs in the Cocktail Bar of the Empress of Britain have delighted admirers, by the thousand, in cities and seaports right round the world, Mr. W. Heath Robinson is an artist of world-acknowledged reputation, both for his serious and his whimsically comic creations. His humorous work appears in periodicals of all the English-speaking countries to say nothing of foreign, since it possesses the quality of merriment at sight that needs no printed word to explain its fun . . . But W. Heath Robinson has also, as an artist, a deep and serious creative vein. His beautiful illustrations of Rudyard Kipling's Song of the English bear this out and he has to his credit many other nobly imagined and delicately executed book illustrations. A modest and entirely unassuming genius, Mr. Heath Robinson is one of three brothers – all artists of repute – who come of a line of artists. In his studio at Highgate, London, he designed and completed on panels of choice and costly woods the whimsical embellishments of the Empress of Britain Cocktail Bar here illustrated.[2]

184 (OPPOSITE) 'A Pleasant Surprise; The Cocktail in the Far East; Clarifying Cocktails; Naming New Cocktails', from *The Story of Cocktails*, 1932.

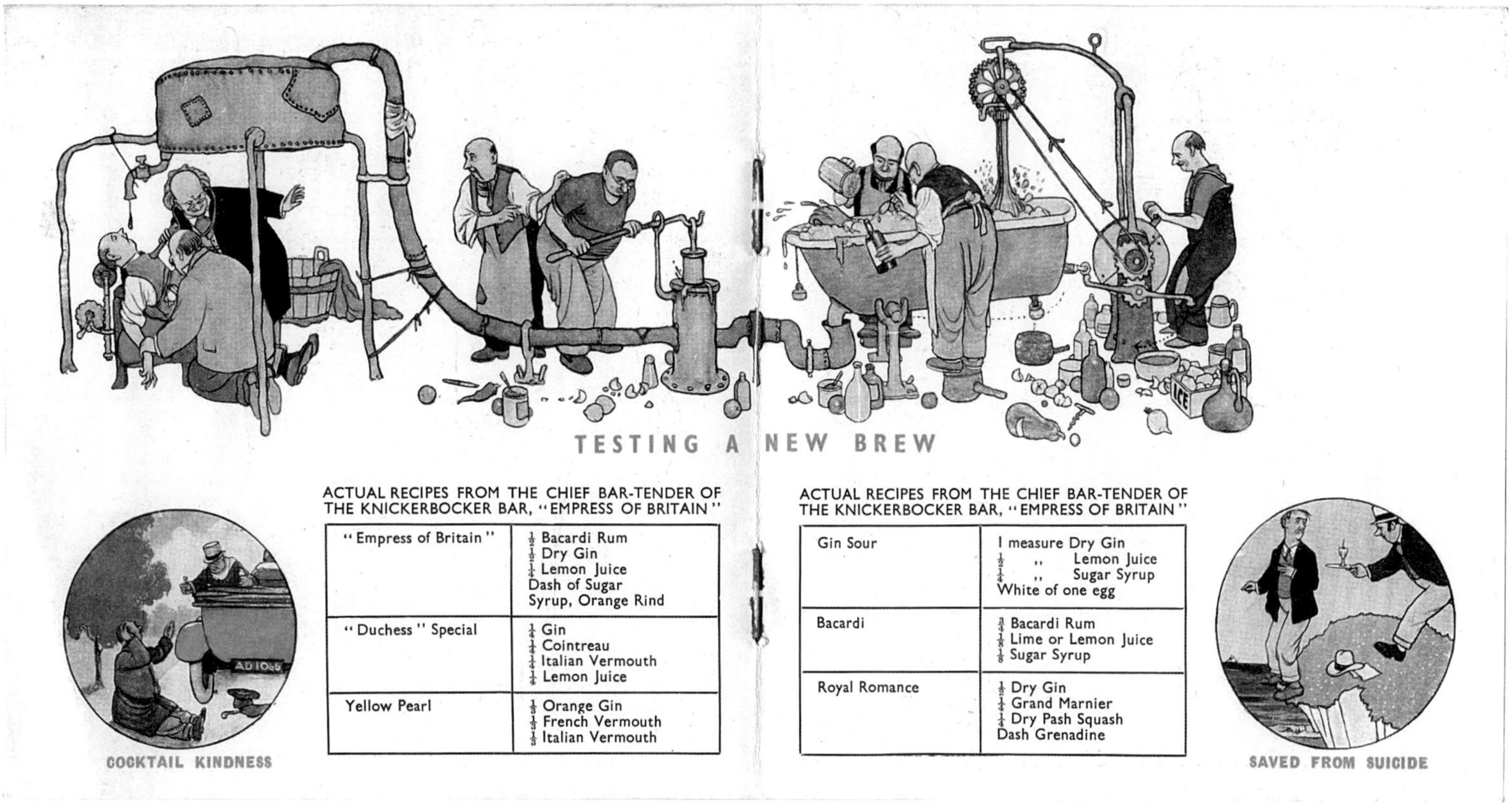

TESTING A NEW BREW
ICE
AD 10
COCKTAIL KINDNESS
SAVED FROM SUICIDE

ACTUAL RECIPES FROM THE CHIEF BAR-TENDER OF THE KNICKERBOCKER BAR, "EMPRESS OF BRITAIN"

"Empress of Britain"	½ Bacardi Rum ½ Dry Gin ¼ Lemon Juice Dash of Sugar Syrup, Orange Rind
"Duchess" Special	¼ Gin ¼ Cointreau ¼ Italian Vermouth ¼ Lemon Juice
Yellow Pearl	⅓ Orange Gin ⅓ French Vermouth ⅓ Italian Vermouth

ACTUAL RECIPES FROM THE CHIEF BAR-TENDER OF THE KNICKERBOCKER BAR, "EMPRESS OF BRITAIN"

Gin Sour	I measure Dry Gin ½ ,, Lemon Juice ¼ ,, Sugar Syrup White of one egg
Bacardi	¾ Bacardi Rum ⅛ Lime or Lemon Juice ⅛ Sugar Syrup
Royal Romance	½ Dry Gin ¼ Grand Marnier ¼ Dry Pash Squash Dash Grenadine

185 'Testing a New Brew', from *The Story of Cocktails*, 1932.

186 Heath Robinson at
work on one of the panels
for the *Empress of Britain*
cocktail bar, 1930/31.

187 Heath Robinson
pouring a cocktail in the
completed 'Knickerbocker'
cocktail bar, 1931.

100 YEARS OF THE GREAT WESTERN RAILWAY

The Great Western Railway was created by an Act of Parliament on 31 August 1835 to provide a double-tracked line from Bristol to London. Construction of the line started in 1836 at two locations: between Bristol and Bath, and Reading and London, eventually closing the gap between them. Grand stations were built at Bristol (Temple Meads), and London (Paddington). The line was completed in 1841. Latterly the company operated a network of bus routes, was a part of the Railway Air Services, and owned ships, docks and hotels.

To celebrate their centenary, GWR commissioned a book of 96 drawings from Heath Robinson (figs 188–94). In his autobiography Heath Robinson recalls:

> In their anxiety that the celebrations should really celebrate, the directors, the heads of the publicity department, the station masters, engine drivers, ticket collectors and all engaged in the working of the railway, naturally turned to me. I joyfully collaborated with a series of drawings published under the title *Railway Ribaldry*. The preparation of these drawings necessitated an intensive study of the history of the Great Western Railway. Besides this, the history of Railway Engineering throughout the country from the days of 'Puffing Billy' (the world's oldest surviving steam locomotive) to the 'Cheltenham Flier' (a GWR train and in 1935 the fastest train in the world) had to be exhaustively considered.[3]

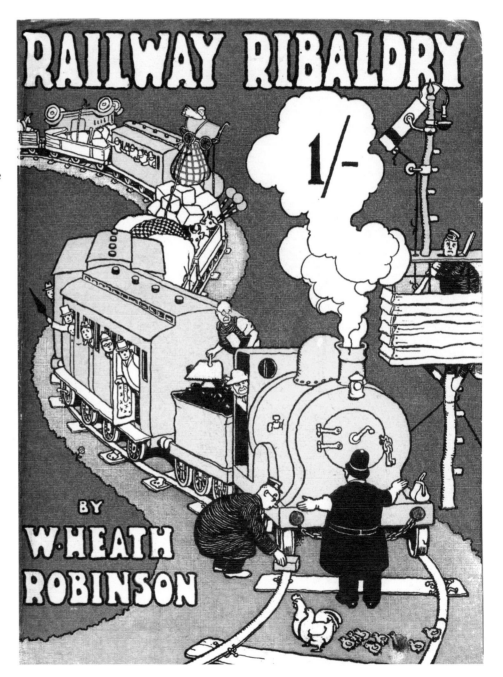

189 'Boring the First Tunnel with
an Early Type of Rotary Excavator',
from *Railway Ribaldry*, 1935.

As usual, Heath Robinson exploited the full
potential of his subject, looking not just at railway
trains and their prototypes, but excursions,
stations, signals, waiting-rooms, booking and lost
property offices, tunnels, sea ferries, railway buses
and – turning to the future – air links and airborne
trains. The peak of the celebrations was reached
when, on a gala excursion, Heath Robinson and
other VIPs were taken, together with 100 of the
company's employees, in a luxurious train from
London to Bristol. Here they met Sir Robert
Horne (the GWR chairman), J.H. Thomas (the
MP for Derby who had started out as an engine
cleaner with the GWR), the Mayor of Bristol, and
many other noted people interested in this great
occasion.

190 'A Very Early Type of Mechanical Signal, Now Rarely to be Seen!', from *Railway Ribaldry*, 1935.

191 'Installing the Electric Telegraph between Paddington and Slough', from *Railway Ribaldry*, 1935.

192 'An Antiquated Method of Filling the Boilers without Stopping the Engine Before the Introduction of the Water Trough System', from *Railway Ribaldry*, 1935.

193 'The Building of the Saltash Bridge', from *Railway Ribaldry*, 1935.

194 'The G.W.R. takes to the air', from *Railway Ribaldry*, 1935.

THEN AND NOW IN THE PORT OF MANCHESTER WAREHOUSES

The Manchester Ship Canal was built in 1894. This 36-mile (58-kilometre) long waterway enabled ocean-going ships to sail right into the Port of Manchester. Two years after the opening of the ship canal, on the canal's banks, the world's first industrial estate was created at Trafford Park. Large quantities of machinery, including cotton processing plant, were exported around the world. Within five years Trafford Park, Europe's largest industrial estate, was home to 40 firms. The earliest structures on the canal side were grain silos; the grain was used for flour and as ballast for ships carrying raw cotton. The Port of Manchester Warehouses Ltd was established in 1914 and was created by Trafford Park Estates to take over the running of its warehousing operations. The warehousing company proved very successful, becoming one of the largest of its type in the country.

Heath Robinson was approached in 1921 to make a series of drawings for a promotional booklet for the company (figs 195–200). It was to be called *Then and Now* and Heath Robinson was to depict how things used to be done before that advent of modern goods handling and cold store equipment. The 'now' side of things was to be illustrated with photographs of the warehouses and their equipment in operation.

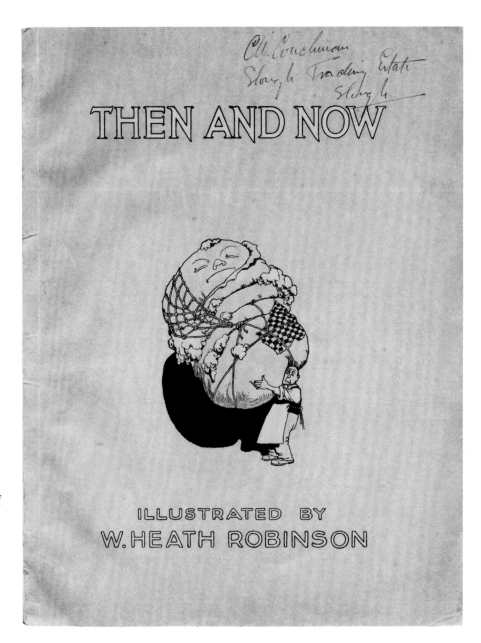

196 'Supposed Origin of the Warehouse – an Early attempt to preserve a filbert', from *Then and Now*, 1921.

197 'An Old and Somewhat Laborious Method of Refrigerating a Fresh Herring', from *Then and Now*, 1921.

198 'Congestion Arising from Manhandling', from *Then and Now*, 1921.

199 'Sectional View of an Old-fashioned Manhandled Warehouse with Storeys', from *Then and Now*, 1921.

200 'A Dream of the Future', from *Then and Now*, 1921.

GARDNER ENGINES

Gardner Engines built a range of diesel-, petrol- and paraffin-fuelled engines at their Barton Hall Works in Patricroft, near Trafford Park, Manchester. Their sales were managed by an associated company, Norris, Henty & Gardners whose main office was in Queen Victoria Street, London. Gardner Engines were taken over by Hawker Siddeley in 1977.

Sometime in 1921, possibly prompted by the success of Heath Robinson's advertising campaign for Port of Manchester Warehouses, they approached A.E. Johnson to commission advertisements for their marine engines. The medium they selected was a set of desk blotters – illustrated cards backed with blotting paper (fig.201). They must have had a fairly limited budget as rather

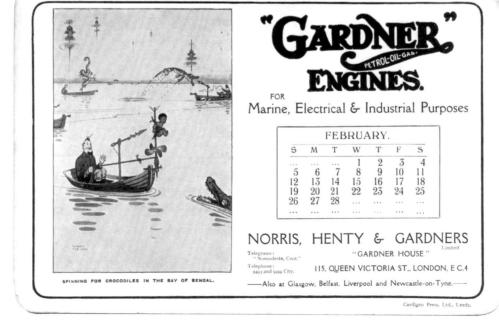

201 'An Old-time Stowaway Disguised as a Figurehead Securing a Free Passage to Margate. + 'Spinning for crocodiles in the bay of Bengal', blotters, 1922.

than having Heath Robinson visit the works and make drawings specially for them, they opted to reuse a variety of humorous drawings that had already been published in magazines. One blotter was produced each month during 1922.

THE WAR IN THE AIR

During the First World War aluminium alloys that retained their strength at high temperatures were developed for use in aero-engines. High Duty Alloys Ltd was founded in 1927 in Slough, Berkshire, using staff and equipment from a bankrupt aero-engine company, on the basis of an order for some thousands of pistons for the Armstrong Siddeley Jaguar aero-engine. Demand from Rolls-Royce later led to expansion into a factory at Redditch. These materials were so crucial to aircraft production that with the outbreak of the Second World War a shadow factory was established in a remote area of Cumberland. The 1,600 torches for the 1948 London Olympics were cast by the company.

In 1941 Heath Robinson was asked to submit ideas for drawings that might be used to advertise the company in the trade press. The theme was to be 'RAF slang', and he produced a set of ten rough sketches. Eight of these were accepted and the finished pictures were published in *Flight* and *The Aeroplane* between September 1941 and June 1942 (figs 202–9). This was his last advertising commission.

202 'No. 1. Blind Flying', from 'The War in the Air' series, published in *Flight*, 11 September 1941.

203 'No. 2. Aero-Camouflage', from 'The War in the Air' series, published in *The Aeroplane*, 12 September 1941.

204 'No. 3. To Bale Out', from 'The War in the Air' series, published in *Flight*, 13 November 1941.

205 'No. 4. The Crate'
from 'The War in the Air'
series, 1941, pen and ink on
paper, 298 × 214 mm
(11¾ × 8½ in).

206 'No. 4. The Crate', from
'The War in the Air' series,
published in *Flight*,
25 December 1941.

207 'No. 6. 1942 Model', from 'The War in the Air' series, published in *Flight*, 19 March 1942.

208 'No. 7. Parachute Landing', from 'The War in the Air' series, published in *Flight*, 30 April 1942.

209 'No. 8. Manoeuvrability', from 'The War in the Air' series, published in *Flight*, 11 June 1942.

8

MOTORING AND CYCLING

I n 1925 Percy Bradshaw, for whom Heath Robinson had briefly worked as a tutor at his Press Art School, wrote *Art in Advertising*, a study of British and American publicity. He discussed the question of whether it was wise to introduce humour into advertising, especially for a company that addresses its publicity to the trade rather than to the public.[1] However, in the example quoted, any doubts were quickly set to rest. A Heath Robinson booklet, issued at a time when business was depressed and customers had forgotten how to smile, met with immediate appreciation, and further material in a similar vein not only received special mention in trade journals at home and abroad, but resulted in a great deal of business. Free editorial publicity generated by the material was in itself valuable, and the booklets even appealed to non-English-speaking customers. Before the booklets were issued the company was faced with the obvious danger that conventional, old-fashioned traders would be offended by such frivolous advertising; but the fear was quite unfounded, as no adverse opinion or criticism of any kind was received. The company in question was Connolly Bros (Curriers) Ltd, but the comments could equally have

applied to any of the 100-plus companies for which Heath Robinson worked at various times.

Heath Robinson embarked on the second major advertising collaboration of his career, with Connolly Bros, in 1920. They were the largest producers of motor hides in Europe at a time when not only the seats of cars, but also their folding hoods, were made of leather. The firm also supplied leather for furniture, bags and cases, harnesses and saddlery and for 'railway use'. Heath Robinson was commissioned to produce a 12-page booklet illustrating various stages in the production of Connolly motor hides for the Motor Show that year. This booklet was called *Nothing Like Leather* and contained six full pages of illustrations, each with an accompanying three-quarter-page line drawing of such subjects as 'the gent who first realised the waterproof nature of cowhide' and 'an early method of skinning a cow'. The title page had a delightful vignette with the caption 'for endurance' and the cover was decorated with four silhouettes illustrating the virtues of leather. These last designs were also employed in an advertisement in a slim booklet of Heath Robinson drawings called *The Home Made Car* the following year. In 1921 Connolly's

210 Detail from *Verkehrte Welt!*, published in *Echo-Continental, c.*1927.

commissioned a similar booklet called from Fougasse, but this proved to be less popular. They therefore returned to Heath Robinson in 1922 and frequently thereafter (figs 211–38).

Amongst the strangest drawings that he made for advertising are those for the house magazine of the German tyre manufacturer Continental (figs 241–46). They include the topsy-turvy world in which motor tyres can only be used on the pavements and a very odd 'Carnival of Laughter'. More conventional was *Technical Talks*, the booklet made for Duckhams showing the making and testing of motor oil.

Cycling rarely features in Heath Robinson's humorous drawings, since it was not an activity that appealed to the well-heeled readers of magazines such as *The Sketch* and *The Bystander*. However, in 1935 he was commissioned to produce one fine full-page coloured drawing for Hercules cycles (fig.240).

LIGHT ON LEATHER

The design of the second Connolly booklet was largely left to the artist, with the stipulation that it should concentrate on the motor industry side of their trade. A.E. Johnson wrote to Heath Robinson at the end of August 1922 asking him to prepare rough sketches for a 24-page booklet, and enclosing some ideas from Denis Murphy, one of the directors, and two samples of their new 'Bedford Cord Hides' which were leather treated to look like fabric. Amongst the ideas offered were the preparation of Morocco grained hides, and the cutting of head-leathers for hoods.

A dummy booklet with rough sketches was delivered to Johnson so that he could decide with Connolly's the size and format required, and on 21 September he wrote to Heath Robinson with details. He also reluctantly advised the artist, who at the time had a very full schedule of work, that:

> it will be absolutely essential for you to come up to town for half a day in order to be taken over Connolly's works again. This is most exasperating, as you are so very busy, and it seems to be totally unnecessary. But, as you know, many of these firms have an idea that nothing can be satisfactorily accomplished until you have been over the works, and the case is particularly acute with Connolly's, because the old man of the firm (a white haired old thing whom you probably met) has got the notion firmly in his head, and is clinging

> to it with the pertinacity of the aged. I did my best to avoid the point, but I can see very clearly that if you do not pay a second visit to the works, the old man in the first place will be convinced that any and every sketch you do is not up to the standard of the first book and not nearly so good as it would have been had you again toured the works: and secondly he will develop the idea that Mr Robinson is not giving to the job as much attention as he ought to. In these circumstances there seems nothing for it but to manage another visit to the works somehow . . . Apart from its being policy to gratify the whim of old Connolly somehow, I think it will save time in the long run to fall in with his wishes. Otherwise he will be making absurd criticisms of every sketch you do, and you will lose more time over alterations etc. than you would gain by not going.

Heath Robinson duly visited the works. On 30 September A.E. Johnson wrote with Connolly's comments on the rough sketches, most of which had been passed. The company's main concern was over the drawings at the head of the foreign-language pages at the end of the booklet, which might 'offend national susceptibilities'. They also wondered whether a more arresting picture could be produced for the front cover. Heath Robinson made the adjustments requested and resubmitted the dummy. On Tuesday 3 October Johnson wrote to say that Connolly's were very pleased with the revised sketches, and asked for the finished drawings 'by first thing on Monday at the latest, and if by any chance you were to get through them before the end of the week, so much the better'. As usual, Heath Robinson delivered on time. Proofs of the booklet were sent on 24 October and the final product, which was called *Light on Leather*, was available for distribution at the Motor Show at the beginning of November (figs 211–17). Once again the booklet was a success and, whilst not quite an annual institution, by 1939 the tally of Heath Robinson booklets for Connolly's was 12, including two collected editions. He also contributed to *Tough Testimonials* in 1924 which included work by ten different artists.

211 The 'more arresting' cover for *Light on Leather*, 1922.

212 'Cutting to Fit in the
Head-leather Department',
from *Light on Leather*, 1922.

213 'Moroccoing Hides in the
Motor Hides Department',
from *Light on Leather*, 1922.

214 'Putting on the Stripes in the Bedford Cord Graining Department', from *Light on Leather*, 1922.

215 'Applying the Perfect Finish in the Antique Hides Department', from *Light on Leather*, 1922.

216 'Obtaining Accurate Measurement in the Measuring Department', from *Light on Leather*, 1922.

217 'Upholsterers at Work with Cushion Hides from Connolly Bros', from *Light on Leather*, 1922.

CONNOLLY BOOKLET COVERS

The covers of five more of the ten booklets that Heath Robinson designed for Connolly's give some idea of the variety of ways he found to present what was essentially the same message many times between 1920 and 1936 (figs 218–23). In addition to the ten separate booklets there were collected editions in 1932 and 1938, the latter reprinted in 1978, and three limited-edition calendars using images from earlier publications in 1989, 1990 and 1991.

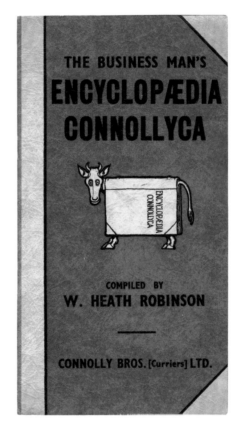

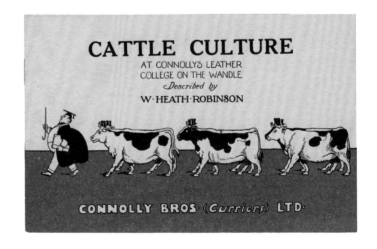

223 Heath Robinson's aerial view of the Connolly works that was inserted as a triple-fold supplement in *Connolly-Land*, 1934.

FEEDING TIME FOR A HERD OF
CUSHION AND SQUAB COWS IN THE
CONNOLLY STOCK YARDS BY THE
UPPER REACHES OF THE RIVER WANDLE

NOTHING TAKES THE PLACE OF LEATHER

LEATHER BREEDING ON THE WANDLE

The booklet produced for the 1927 Motor Show was called *Leather Breeding on the Wandle* (figs 224–31). In it Heath Robinson imagined that the different finishes for Connolly hides were produced by breeding cattle with the required characteristics, rather than by the industrial tanning processes.

224 'Feeding Time for a Herd of Cushion and Squab Cows', from *Leather Breeding on the Wandle*, 1927.

225 *Leather Breeding on the Wandle* cover, 1927.

TRAINING THE HIDES OF YOUNG
CALVES TO ACQUIRE THE FAMOUS
SELF-PLEATING FINISH

W. HEATH ROBINSON.

NOTHING TAKES THE PLACE OF LEATHER

Members of Con-
nolly's staff of beauty
specialists at work on
a cow to preserve
that perfect softness
for which Connolly's
leather is so famous.

226 'Training the Hides of Young Calves to acquire the Famous
Self-pleating Finish', from *Leather Breeding on the Wandle*, 1927.

227 'Members of Connolly's Staff of Beauty Specialists at Work . . .',
from *Leather Breeding on the Wandle*, 1927.

TENDING A HERD OF ANNO DOMINI
COWS SPECIALLY BRED AND
PRESERVED FOR THE ANTIQUE
FINISH ACQUIRED BY THEIR HIDES

NOTHING TAKES THE PLACE OF LEATHER

228 'Tending a Herd of Anno Domini Cows', from *Leather Breeding on the Wandle*, 1927.

SELECTING A PERFECT HIDE FROM
ONE OF CONNOLLY'S HERDS OF HOOD
HEIFERS FOR A SPECIAL EXHIBIT AT
THE MOTOR SHOW

NOTHING TAKES THE PLACE OF LEATHER

229 'Selecting a Perfect Hide', from *Leather Breeding on the Wandle*, 1927.

230 'Inuring the Hides of a Herd of Connolly's Famous Cushion Cows . . .', from *Leather Breeding on the Wandle*, 1927.

INURING THE HIDES OF A HERD OF CONNOLLY'S FAMOUS CUSHION COWS TO THE HARD WEAR TO WHICH THEY WILL BE SUBJECTED AS MOTOR CAR AND FURNITURE UP-HOLSTERY LEATHER

NOTHING TAKES THE PLACE OF LEATHER

231 'Accustoming the Hides of Some of Connolly's Famous Herd of Water-proof Cattle', from *Leather Breeding on the Wandle*, 1927.

ACCUSTOMING THE HIDES OF SOME OF CONNOLLY'S FAMOUS BREED OF WATER-PROOF CATTLE TO THE RESISTANCE OF WATER —INSIDE AND OUT.

NOTHING TAKES THE PLACE OF LEATHER

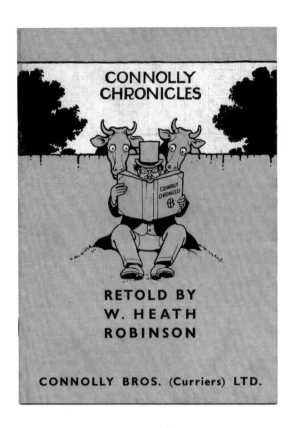

CONNOLLY CHRONICLES

For the 1933 Motor Show booklet Heath Robinson was at his most inventive, with a series of drawings showing the benefits of Connolly leather in a historical setting and the modern equivalent situation (figs 232–8). In the first picture, Mr and Mrs Noah find comfortable seats on the cows while their modern counterparts have leather-upholstered fireside chairs. On the wall are a pair of birds in cages, while outside it is pouring with rain. In another pair of drawings, King John loses his treasure in The Wash because he did not pack it securely in leather. His modern counterpart, a well-heeled gentleman, travels safe in the knowledge that his belongings are packed in leather luggage. A less fortunate travelling companion loses his goods as his paper parcel falls apart.

232 *Connolly Chronicles*
cover, 1933.

233 'Mr & Mrs Noah Always Found the Most Comfortable
Seats in the Ark', from *Connolly Chronicles*, 1933.

HISTORY REPEATS ITSELF

HISTORY REPEATS ITSELF

234 'Tutankhamen Finds it More Convenient and Less Tiring to Go into Battle Seated on Leather', from *Connolly Chronicles*, 1933.

235 'King Alfred was Glad he had Remembered to Don his Leather Jerkin', from *Connolly Chronicles*, 1933.

WILLIAM THE CONQUEROR
APPRECIATES THE COMFORTS OF
LEATHER WHEN CROSSING THE CHANNEL

CONNOLLY COMFORT

HISTORY REPEATS ITSELF

236 'William the Conqueror Appreciates the Comforts of Leather when Crossing the Channel', from *Connolly Chronicles*, 1933.

237 'What Would Not Have Happened to King John in the Wash if Only He Had Packed in Real Leather', from *Connolly Chronicles*, 1933.

238 'Drake is in His Hammock – A thousand miles away', from *Connolly Chronicles*, 1933.

THE DAIMLER WAY OF ENSURING QUALITY

Daimler started building cars in England in 1896. Shortly after the First World War Daimler asked Heath Robinson to make a set of four drawings illustrating their quality control processes. One is shown here (fig.239). The other titles were 'The Laboratory', 'Daimler's Test Shop for Chassis and Cars' and 'Daimler's Paint Shop'. They were used in a publication issued by Daimler in 1920, entitled *The Daimler Way of Ensuring Quality*.

239 'Daimler's Engine Testing Shop', from *The Daimler Way of Ensuring Quality*, 1920.

THE WEEKEND ALL-WEATHER TANDEM

The Hercules Cycle and Motor Company Ltd was founded in September 1910 at Aston in Birmingham, making bicycles and, later, mopeds. By offering good quality at keen prices, the company prospered and by the 1930s it had become the world's biggest cycle manufacturer.

To show off their products, Hercules published elaborate catalogues that they called magazines, enlivened with articles and drawings, which were distributed to potential customers through retail outlets. For the *Hercules Cycle Magazine* of 1935 they requested a feature from Heath Robinson on the advantages of a tandem. He responded enthusiastically with a full-page storyboard depicting a tandem so splendidly equipped that it could transport and shelter a family of three on a camping weekend, come rain or come shine (fig.240).

In the 1960s the company was swallowed up in the British Cycle Corporation, and that was the end of the Hercules name.

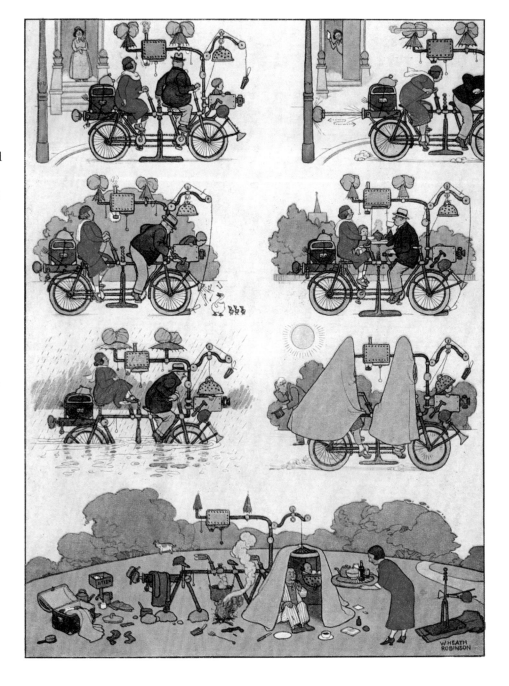

240 'A Perfect Picnic on the Week-End All-Weather Tandem', published in *Hercules Cycle Magazine*, 1935.

CONTINENTAL TYRES

Continental was founded in Hanover, Germany, in 1871 as a rubber manufacturer, Continental-Caoutchouc und Gutta-Percha Compagnie. They started making car tyres in 1898, and in 1904 made the world's first car tyre with a patterned tread. Continental is now the world's fourth-largest tyre manufacturer.

Erich Maria Remarque, author of the 1929 novel *All Quiet on the Western Front*, worked for Continental Rubber as a test driver and as an editor and writer of humour and verse for the in-house magazine, *Echo Continental*. It is not known how Heath Robinson's work came to Remarque's attention, but the artist made two surreal drawings for *Echo Continental* (figs 241–2). In 1928 he also produced designs for a series of eight postcards – some for distribution in England (figs 243–4) and others for use in Germany (figs 245–6). The captions on the German cards are much more poetic and imaginative. The German examples reproduced here are covered with close-packed writing in pencil on both sides.

241 'Verkehrte Welt!' [Topsy-Turvy World!], published in *Echo-Continental*, *c.*1927.

So stelit sich der humorvolle Zeichner W. Heath Robinson den Straßenverkehr vor, wenn nach einer Polizeiverfügung die Bereifung der Fahrstraße auf den Fußsteig verpflanzt würde.

Sicherlich zu des einen Freud, des anderen Leid.

[The humorist W. Heath Robinson imagines road traffic if, after a police order, the tyres from the road are switched with those from the pavement. Certainly one man's joy is another man's sorrow.]

242 'Horch! Paukenschlag und Drommetenstoß!...'

[Listen! Drumbeat and trumpet call!'...], published in *Echo-Continental*, c.1927.

Stolz reitet der König auf »Conti« hier, Gefolgt von dem schwarzen Rittertroß, Zum lachenden Kampf, zum — Faschingsturnier!

[Proudly the king rides forth on 'Conti', followed by the black knight's retinue, to the carnival tournament of laughter.]

3. Filling a "Middle - Age" tyre during a rough passage of the royal family.

The evolution of the "Continental Tyre"

5. With the Continental Giant Pneumatic you are "at home" on the road at all times.

The evolution of the "Continental Tyre"

243 'Filling a 'Middle-Age' tyre during a rough passage for the Royal Family', postcard, 1928.

244 'With the Continental Giant Pneumatic you are "at home" on the road at all times', postcard, 1928.

DAS TANZ-BILLIARD-ÜBERLAND-RESTAURANT-AUTOMOBIL.

Einst tanzte man im Auto, aber unfreiwillig, weil das ganze Auto tanzte,
wenn es über holprige Straßen fuhr. Wenn man dagegen heute durch
die Lande fährt, und der Wagen auf weichen „Conti-Riesenluftreifen"
dahingleitet, als ob er den Boden nicht berührte, dann tanzt höchstens
das Herz im Leib.

DIE REIFEN-PRÜFMASCHINE.

Auf dieser sinnreichen Maschine wird jeder Contireifen geprüft, ehe er
die Fabrik verläßt. Erst wenn er seine Zuverlässigkeit erwiesen hat,
wenn weder der Klingelapparat in Bewegung gesetzt, noch die Pulver-
fässer in die Luft geflogen sind, dann — aber erst dann — wird der
Reifen für den Gebrauch freigegeben.

245 'Das Tanze-Billiard-Oberland-Restaurant-Automobil' [The Dance-Billiards-Overland-Restaurant-Vehicle], postcard, 1928.

[Once you danced in the car involuntarily, because the whole car danced when it drove over bumpy roads. However today, driving through the countryside with 'Conti – giant pneumatic tyre', the car glides away as if it did not touch the ground, and then the heart dances up into the body.]

246 'Die Reifen-Prufemaschine' [The Tyre Testing Machine], postcard, 1928.

[In this ingenious machine every Conti tyre is tested before it leaves the factory. Only when its reliability has been proved, if neither the bells ring, nor the barrels of powder explode, then – but only then – the tyre is approved for use.]

9

FOR THE SMOKER

From the outbreak of the First World War the production of gift books was gradually stifled by increasing restrictions and the shortage of paper, and by the end of the war the market for such books had disappeared. Heath Robinson had therefore to depend entirely on the humorous side of his work for his income. His wartime cartoons had proved immensely popular with servicemen overseas and with his readers at home, and so he was greatly in demand with magazine editors.

His first major advertising project since Lamson Paragon was for R.J. Lea Ltd of Manchester, to advertise their 'Chairman' tobacco. This took the form of a series of 12 humorous pen-and-wash drawings illustrating the 12 virtues of 'Chairman' (figs 7 and 247–54). Undoubtedly, Heath Robinson had a hand in selecting the virtues to be illustrated, for whilst some are those that would obviously occur to any advertising agent, others betray the artist's unique style of humour. The manufacturer himself would have insisted on promoting its attractive aroma, the entire absence of burning sensation, that it suits most palates, and that it is an economy. He would have been unlikely to have suggested that it

is 'a solace to the very end' or insisted on promoting 'its taking qualities'; and only Heath Robinson could have suggested that 'it promotes Mark Tapleyism'. These drawings appeared in *Punch* and *London Opinion* at roughly monthly intervals between July 1915 and June 1916. A 13th drawing, illustrating 'A Chairman Calamity', was made for use in the special Christmas numbers of these magazines in 1915 (fig.255). It is interesting to note that whilst Heath Robinson had 13 full-page cartoons published in the advertising pages of *Punch* during this one 12-month period, the sum total of his work in the editorial sections of that magazine throughout his career amounted to one full-page line drawing and seven vignettes.

Heath Robinson's younger brother George had set up as a publisher with a partner called John Birch. The enterprise seems to have been only marginally successful, and George was not ashamed to ask his more successful and more famous brothers for help. In 1920 he prevailed on William to make a series of drawings for a publication called *Get On With It* (figs 256–7). A page of vignette drawings by Heath Robinson shows 'more unsolicited testimonials' for

247 Detail from 'The Twelve Virtues of Chairman, No. 2. – A solace to the very end', published in *Punch*, 11 August 2015.

De Reszke cigarettes (fig.258). One of De Reszke's coloured advertisements shows a sophisticated couple on a golf course drawn by Reginald Higgins. Four of the Heath Robinson vignettes were later used in a booklet of testimonials titled *Applause*.

Heath Robinson also made drawings for press advertisements for Kensitas cigarettes and for a promotional booklet for Oppenheimer, the first makers of pipes from briar root.

THE TWELVE VIRTUES OF CHAIRMAN TOBACCO

R.J. Lea was founded in 1865 and manufactured tobacco and cigarettes at 45 Market Street and Broughton Lane, Manchester. Later they moved to Stockport. Their popular brands were 'Chairman', 'Tournament' and Lea's 'Honeydew' and 'Navy Cut'. 'Vice Chair' was introduced around 1910. The firm was taken over by John Sinclair in 1937.

Heath Robinson's drawings illustrating *The Twelve Virtues of Chairman Tobacco* (figs 7 and 247–54) were a departure for a company whose previous advertisements had featured either their products or elderly gentlemen in period dress representing 'The Chairman'. The drawings are in the style of his contemporary cartoons in *The Sketch* and other periodicals and, in both concept and execution, match the best of them. They contain a wealth of amusing detail in addition to the main subject, often involving the already famous Heath Robinson birds or other animals. In 'Its Attractive Aroma', the first of the series (fig.248), an elderly man is sitting at an open window smoking 'Chairman' and reading his newspaper, while an airman lowers himself on a knotted string to steal a puff from the pipe. Above, a small bird is stretching its neck over the coping to inhale the rising smoke. The second, illustrating 'A Solace to the Very End' (fig.247), shows the pipe smoker disappearing down the throat of a crocodile, a contented smile on his face. In these drawings the streak of surrealism, that was later suppressed by editors careful of the sensibilities of their readers, is evident.

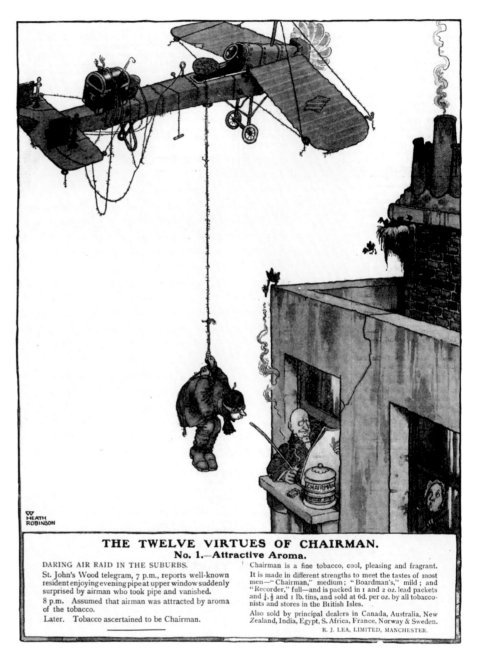

248 'The Twelve Virtues of Chairman, No. 1. – Attractive Aroma', published in *Punch*, 14 July 1915.

THE TWELVE VIRTUES OF CHAIRMAN.
No. 3.—Entire absence of burning sensation.

When preparing for a dinner you have no wish to attend the wonderful coolness of Chairman is most comforting—as welcome to the smoker as it is unexpected by those who do not know it.

Those who smoke Chairman have the best that tobacco can give, and to those who newly try it it brings an unlooked for pleasure, as its continued enjoyment is not gained at the cost of a burned tongue.

In all ways it is a fine tobacco, with a pleasing aroma, an attractive flavour, and a peculiar coolness that is as un-usual as it is essential to the complete enjoyment of the pipe.

It is made in different strengths to meet the tastes of most men—" Chairman," medium; " Boardman's," mild; and " Recorder," full—and is packed in one and **2 oz.** lead packets and $\frac{1}{4}$, $\frac{1}{2}$, and 1-lb. tins, and sold at 6d. **per oz.** by all tobacconists and stores in the British Isles.

Also sold by principal dealers in Canada, Australia, New Zealand, India, Egypt, S. Africa, France, Norway and Sweden.

R. J. LEA, LIMITED, MANCHESTER.

249 'The Twelve Virtues of Chairman, No. 3. – Entire absence of burning sensation', published in *Punch*, 8 September 1915.

In November 1915 Heath Robinson received a letter from a young lieutenant with the Mediterranean Expeditionary Force in the Dardanelles who wrote:

Dear Mr. Heath Robinson,
I trust you will excuse me writing to you in this fashion, but I have just received from home *Punch* of the 20th October, & have spent the greater part of the evening enjoying your advertisement for Chairman Tobacco. It is the best thing in *Punch* & one of the most priceless of your priceless drawings.

I know it is rather an impertinent request, but I should deem it a very great honour if you would let me have an autographed drawing by yourself.

The drawing referred to was 'No. 4 — Fragrance which all enjoy' (fig.250).

THE TWELVE VIRTUES OF CHAIRMAN.
No. 4.—Fragrance which all enjoy.

The smoking of Chairman is a kindly and pleasing habit, gratifying to others as well as to the smoker himself. Those who are barred from its direct enjoyment can share its pleasures when opportunity permits.

With it the pipe is no longer banned from sitting-room and lounge nor consigned to the outer darkness of the garden or the solitude of the study.

Its pleasing flavour and fine fragrance may be enjoyed on all occasions when the pipe is permissible and always with satisfaction, for it does not burn the tongue.

It is made in different strengths to meet the tastes of most men—"Chairman," medium; "Boardman's," mild; and "Recorder," full — and is sold at 8d. per oz. in 1 and 2 oz. lead packets, and at 2/7 per ¼-lb. in ¼, ½ and 1 lb. tins, by all leading tobacconists and stores.

Also sold by principal dealers in Canada, Australia, New Zealand, India, Egypt, S. Africa, France, Norway and Sweden.

R. J. LEA, LIMITED, MANCHESTER.

250 'The Twelve Virtues of Chairman, No. 4. – Fragrance which all enjoy', published in *Punch*, 20 October 1915.

THE TWELVE VIRTUES OF CHAIRMAN.
No. 6.—Promotes geniality.

The virtues of Chairman are very real. It is most improbable that the genial and friendly feeling depicted above, or even the good fellowship of less unusual occasions, would be born of a poor or ordinary tobacco. The right atmosphere is created only by the best that tobacco has to give. That is Chairman.

And there is economy in it also. The difference in cost between Chairman and an ordinary tobacco—even a low-priced tobacco—is a few pence a week at the most. But the difference in satisfaction is so much greater that it far outweighs this small extra cost. It means an added pleasure with every pipe. Hours of it. Actually about six hours to the ounce, which makes Chairman one of the least costly but most real and satisfying of the little pleasures of life.

Chairman is medium in strength, with a pleasing flavour and aroma and always cool to the tongue. Boardman's is the same tobacco milder, and Recorder the same but fuller flavoured.

These three brands are sold by all leading tobacconists and stores at 8d. per oz. in 1 and 2 oz. lead packets, and at 2/7 per ¼-lb. in ¼, ½ and 1-lb. tins.

Also sold by principal dealers in France, Norway, Sweden, India, Canada, Egypt, S. Africa, New Zealand, and the Far East.

R. J. LEA LIMITED, MANCHESTER.

251 'The Twelve Virtues of Chairman, No. 6. – Promotes geniality', published in *Punch*, 8 December 1915.

THE TWELVE VIRTUES OF CHAIRMAN.

No. 9.—Banishes Discomfort and brings Content.

A pipe of Chairman is most excellent smoking at **all times,** but never are its virtues more potent than **when discomfort** reigns—its soothing influence brings a **cheerful content in its train.** It pleases the palate with its **flavour and its** clean and fragrant aroma is a delight which others **than the** smoker may enjoy.

The pleasures it gives are constant with **every pipe no** matter how much it may be smoked, as it is always **cool to** the tongue and burns sweetly to the last shred.

In these days of higher taxation it is an economy, **as it costs** less than either cigars or cigarettes of satisfying quality.

Each ounce yields a full six hours of enjoyment and costs but eightpence.

It is made in different strengths to meet the tastes of most men—" Chairman," medium ; " Boardman's," mild ; and " Recorder," full—and is sold at 8d. per oz. in 1 and 2 oz. lead packets, and at 2/7 per ¼-lb. in ¼, ½ and 1-lb. tins by all principal tobacconists and stores.

Also sold by principal dealers in Canada, Australia, New Zealand, India, Egypt, S. Africa, France, Norway, Sweden and the Far East.

R. J. LEA, LIMITED, MANCHESTER.

252 'The Twelve Virtues of Chairman, No. 9. – Banishes Discomfort and brings Content', published in *Punch*, 8 March 1916.

CHAIRMAN
W HEATH ROBINSON
THE TWELVE VIRTUES OF CHAIRMAN.
No. 10.—It suits most palates.
There is a very unusual attractiveness about Chairman. It pleases the palate with its coolness and flavour, and it has an aroma which appeals to most people whether they are smokers or not. As a pipe tobacco it has no superior.
Also at the present time, especially, it is an economy, being cheaper than either cigarettes or cigars of a quality which can possibly satisfy, as it provides six hours of the best smoking to the ounce.
It is made in different strengths to meet the tastes of most men—"Chairman," medium; "Boardman's," mild; and "Recorder," full—and is sold at 8d. per oz. in 1 and 2 oz. lead packets, and at 2/7 per ¼-lb. in ¼, ½ and 1-lb. tins by all principal tobacconists and stores.
Also sold by principal dealers in Canada, Australia, New Zealand, India, Egypt, S. Africa, France, Norway, Sweden and the Far East.
R. J. LEA, LIMITED, MANCHESTER.

253 'The Twelve Virtues of Chairman, No. 10. – It suits most palates', published in *Punch*, 12 April 1916.

A CHAIRMAN CALAMITY

The series of 12 virtues was followed by one more advertisement that was published in both *Punch* and *London Opinion* (fig.255). It was perhaps the first of a succession of humorous drawings in which Heath Robinson divides the page, with the upper portion showing what is happening above the water and the remainder activities underwater.

THE TWELVE VIRTUES OF CHAIRMAN.

No. 11.—It promotes Mark Tapleyism.

When through unkind circumstances one is plunged into the midst of troubles, a pipe of Chairman is very comforting. It buoys up the feelings, and helps one to take a more cheerful view of things. For it is a fine tobacco that yields the greatest pleasure that the votary of the pipe may experience. It is cool to the tongue, fragrant in its burning, and with a flavour that pleases with every pipe. It neither palls on the palate nor loses its charm, but is a sure source of pleasure month in and month out.

At the present time it is especially an economy, yielding six hours of the best smoking to the ounce.

It is made in different strengths to meet the tastes of most men—" Chairman," medium; " Boardman's," mild; and " Recorder," full—and is sold at 8d. per oz. in 1 and 2 oz. lead packets, and at 2/7 per ½-lb. in ¼, ½ and 1-lb. canisters by all principal tobacconists and stores.

Also sold by principal dealers in Canada, Australia, New Zealand, India, Egypt, S. Africa, France, Norway, Sweden and the Far East.

R. J. LEA, LIMITED, MANCHESTER.

254 'The Twelve Virtues of Chairman, No. 11. – It promotes Mark Tapleyism', published in *Punch*, 10 May 1916.

[This virtue refers to the character Mark Tapley in Charles Dickens's *The Life and Adventures of Martin Chuzzlewit* (1842–4) who was only content when facing hardship. Only then could he display his qualities of fortitude and cheerfulness in all circumstances.]

A Chairman Calamity.

This is the wholly misleading drawing that the artist supplied. His collaborator, the man of words and phrases, would have nothing to do with it. It worried him. He could not find a useful argument for his purpose in the tubby turbot, the confiding crab or the savoury sardine. Nor did the submersible smoker, the curious chicken—or should it be the searching seagull?—inspire him with words to convey the fact that the illustration is intended to emphasise the perfect combustion of Chairman.

So it is left for the commercial man to say that this quality is responsible for the intense and delightful coolness of his tobacco and ensures its delicate flavour and pleasing aroma being enjoyed with every pipe however much it may be smoked.

Chairman Tobacco is made in three strengths—Chairman, medium; "Boardman's," mild; "Recorder," full—and is sold by all leading tobacconists and stores at 8d. per oz. in 1 and 2 oz. lead packets, and at 2/7 per ¼-lb. in ¼, ½ and 1 lb. tins.

Also sold by principal dealers in France, Norway, Sweden, India, Canada, Egypt, S. Africa, Australia, New Zealand, and the East.

R. J. LEA, LIMITED, MANCHESTER.

255 'A Chairman Calamity', published in *Punch Almanack* for 1916.

256 *Get On With It* cover, 1920.

257 'The Latest Machine for Tipping Matches with Phosphorus (amorphous or non-poisonous)', from *Get On With It*, 1920.

GET ON WITH IT

In about 1920 Heath Robinson's younger brother George, in partnership with J. Birch, embarked on a career in publishing and advertising from offices at 17 Tooks Court, close to Chancery Lane, in London. Their first publication was *Get On With It*, a one-off magazine-style booklet designed around a series of double-page advertisements. It had a two-page introduction, 16 full-page cartoons and 36 line drawings by Heath Robinson in addition to one double-page and one full-page advertisement by him. Most of the advertisers used their standard press advertisements. The full-page cartoon on tipping matches shown here (fig.257) was followed by a double-page advertisement for Bryant & May's matches.

SOME UNSOLICITED TESTIMONIALS FOR DE RESZKE CIGARETTES

De Reszke cigarettes were manufactured by J. Millhoff & Co. Ltd. When the drawing shown here was published in *Get On With It* in 1920 (fig.258), it was faced by an advertisement for De Reszke cigarettes, one of a series drawn by Reginald Higgins. (Note that the lady with the cat says 'j'adore les cigarettes de mon Millhoff'.) A year later Millhoff published a little book, titled *Applause*, containing celebrity testimonials and in it they reproduced four of the vignettes from Heath Robinson's drawing. Two years after that, they employed Heath Robinson to make a small advertising drawing as part of a feature in the 27 July issue of the *Evening News* (fig.180).

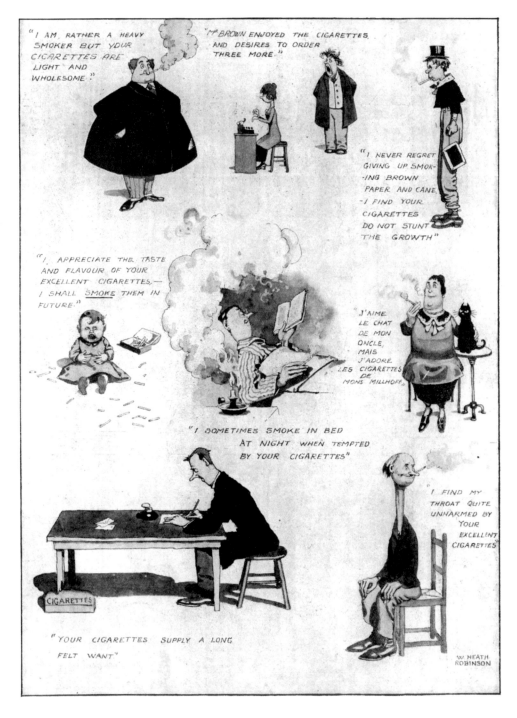

258 'More Unsolicited Testimonials', from *Get On With It*, 1920.

10

BUSINESS AND FINANCE

M oney and the business of financial management rarely appear in Heath Robinson's humorous work for magazines. There are scenes of 'Working overtime at the Mint' and 'A busy morning at the Bank of England', but little else. His advertising career had started with the drawings that he made for Lamson Paragon, whose business was to support the retail trade and in particular to help them control their cash flow. The project led to an enduring friendship with John Meath Evans, who had started as advertising manager for the company and ended up as its managing director; but when the project ended in 1907, Heath Robinson returned to his demanding twin careers of illustrator and cartoonist. As the market for finely illustrated books all but dried up during the First World War and he looked again to advertising for employment, it was tobacco and whisky that he was asked to promote.

With the end of the war companies were clamouring for the services of the artist who had done so much to raise the morale of the servicemen and the public at home. Near the front of the queue was the Burroughs Adding Machine Company.

They wanted a series of small line drawings that could be printed on desk blotters. The subject would be the problems that office machinery could ease and the benefits that it might bring. It seemed to be a relatively straightforward commission, but a top-heavy management structure, with a number of department heads all having an opinion, made it slow and tedious to complete. On the plus side, we are left with a highly original and amusing set of drawings (figs 264–73).

The set of drawings that Heath Robinson made for the turf accountant Douglas Stuart in 1935 (figs 260–63) hark back to his earliest Lamson Paragon work (figs 5 and 274–80). His mechanical inventions were inappropriate to the subject, as was a historical treatment. He chose instead to revive the method of working that he had used in his earliest advertising commissions with Chas. Ed. Potter and John Meath Evans. This was to take a catchphrase and to illustrate it in a humorous way, often by taking an over-literal interpretation of the words used.

His only other forays into the world of finance were two small press advertisements that were part of a double-page advertising supplement in the

259 Detail of 'Old Methods of Calculating Costs', from *Two and Two Make Four*, c.1924.

Evening Standard on New Year's Day 1934 headed 'Heath Robinson Brings in the New Year with Good Resolutions' (fig.179). The two companies featured were the Cooperative Permanent Building Society and the Prudential Assurance Company Ltd. For the former his drawing shows the perils of trying to build your own house. For the Prudential he has designed a complicated piece of machinery that will tell you 'at a glance' the position of your insurance.

THE TURF ACCOUNTANT FOR YOU

Each of the drawings that Heath Robinson made for Douglas Stuart had one or more horses in it. References to such racing terms as 'putting a monkey' on a horse or 'backing a horse in your own home' inspired some of the artist's most inventive and witty drawings of his later years (figs 260–63). A total of eight drawings were published between January 1936 and April 1937, appearing on the back covers of the *Illustrated Sporting and Dramatic News* and the *Illustrated London News*, and most were used two or three times.

260 'If You Must Have Something On, Tell "Duggie" all about it', published in *Illustrated London News*, 27 June 1936.

261 'When Getting a Tip Straight from the Horse's Mouth – Tell "Duggie" all about it', published in *Illustrated Sport and Dramatic News*, 14 February 1936.

262 'When Backing a
Horse in Your Own Home
– Tell "Duggie" all about it',
published in *Illustrated Sport
and Dramatic News*,
21 February 1936.

263 'If You Are About to
Put a "Monkey" on a Horse
. . . Tell "Duggie" all about it',
published in *Illustrated Sport
and Dramatic News*,
26 February 1936.

THE DAWN OF THE IDEA
THAT 2 + 2 = 4

W. HEATH ROBINSON

PATENT
COMBINATION
MACHINE
For levelling up
matters at the
end of the year

W. HEATH ROBINSON

THE BENEFITS OF BURROUGHS' ADDING MACHINES

In 1921 Heath Robinson was approached by Burroughs Adding Machine Company to make some drawings for a booklet. He prepared a rough dummy which was sent to the firm, but nothing further was heard for some time. Then the company decided that what it wanted was 12 small line drawings to make up a series of blotters, each of which would also bear a date block for a month of the year. The fee for this work was to be one hundred guineas. It was a condition of the project that he 'should not guy the machine itself', but should burlesque various aspects of office routine, and particularly book-keeping. Only three of the original subjects from the dummy booklet were approved for use on blotters. The new commission was received on 22 November and the aim was to get the blotters out in time for the New Year, so time was short. The first task was to get rough sketches approved for the remaining nine designs. On 11 January 1922 four more of the designs were approved. The January blotter had already been printed, but two of the four were required urgently as the February and March blotters were to be printed at the same time.

On 27 January 1922, Heath Robinson received a letter from his agent A.E. Johnson, saying:

The unfortunate printer who has that Burroughs Adding Machine business in hand is again agitating for more drawings. I understand that the Burroughs people have been so fussy and dilatory that they have only themselves to blame for the delay. I don't think therefore that you need put undue stress upon yourself to push these drawings forward, but at the same time if you can hasten them without too much inconvenience to yourself, so much the better.

Another sketch was approved on 3 February, with the news that 'The unfortunate printer is tearing his hair with anxiety'. On 7 February Johnson's

264 'The Dawn of the Idea that 2 + 2 = 4', from *Two and Two Make Four*, c.1924.

265 'Patent Combination Machine', from *Two and Two Make Four*, c.1924.

W. HEATH
ROBINSON

FOURPENCE
OUT
Awkward predicament of ill-equipped office on finding the balance out

266 'Fourpence Out', from *Two and Two Make Four*, c.1924.

assistant J.W. Boot wrote: 'I have just been asked by the printers if you would introduce the office cat assisting the staff in one of the drawings you have in hand entitled "Making out the Statements". Apparently in some offices everybody in the building is called in to assist.' Two weeks later, Heath Robinson was asked to further alter the drawing:

although they like it immensely, they wonder if you would mind making it a little more busy by placing another list of statements on the wall, and another boy on the ladder calling down to the man writing on the floor. Also they had great hopes that when you put the cat in, it would be helping in the accounts, and they would be awfully obliged if you would make the animal sticking down envelopes, or some similar occupation.

On 4 April he heard from Johnson that changes were required to two more of his drawings:

I send you herewith one of the Burroughs Adding Machine sketches, 'The Clever Lad'. Attached to it you will find [a] proof illustration of one of Burroughs' machines. They want you to re-draw the machine which the Clever Lad is holding behind his back rather more in accordance with the proof illustration. As you will see, the actual machine is somewhat different in shape and appearance from the one that you have drawn.

At the same time they want you to compare the face of the schoolmaster in the drawing with the same face shown in your rough sketch, which I presume you still have. The Burroughs people appear to think that the face in the rough sketch is better than the face in the finished drawing. Perhaps you could alter it accordingly.

The rough sketch for 'Autre Temps' has been turned down. I enclose the remarks of the head of the Burroughs Advertising Department. A rough sketch is wanted on the lines of these.

At the same time it is desired to see again all the many roughs which you have already done. There is apparently some talk of the Burroughs people wanting a further series, and it is possible that they would pick some subjects from those previously rejected roughs.

I don't know how you feel about this Burroughs business, and whether you would care to undertake another series. The price they are paying is not a bad one for these small drawings, but I fear you must have suffered considerable irritation from the extreme difficulty in giving satisfaction. The trouble is, of course, that your sketches are passed round to the heads of half a dozen different departments. One can never get agreement in that way at the best of times, and moreover probably each departmental head feels it incumbent on him to make some suggestion or criticism, just to show that he is earning his salary.

I therefore propose in regard to a further series to lay it down that once this preliminary

A PRIMITIVE FORM OF MACHINE USED IN STOCK -TAKING: REGISTERING THE AMOUNT OF SUGAR ON HAND

LOAF SUGAR

INK

HEATH ROBINSON

267 'A Primitive Form of Machine Used in Stock Taking', from *Two and Two Make Four*, c.1924.

series of twelve is out of the way, you are not prepared to undertake any more unless they agree to pay you a fee of, say, one guinea, for every rough sketch which they ask you to submit. This would put a curb on their critical faculties, or if not, at least make the job worthwhile.

There were enquiries about a further series, with the proposal of a second set based on the titles of Shakespeare plays 'as long as the comic interpretation has some bearing on the routine work of an office'. Nothing came of this.

However, following the publication of the blotters, Burroughs received many requests for: 'further copies of some of the Cartoons drawn for us by Mr. W. Heath Robinson and circulated as Monthly Calendar Blotters during 1922.' The company responded by publishing a booklet that combined the drawings with endorsements of the claims of Burroughs Adding, Book-keeping and Calculating Machines. The booklet included nine of the 12 original drawings (figs 264–72).

268 'Posting from Day Books to Ledger', from *Two and Two Make Four*, c.1924.

269 'Making Out a Monthly Statement',
from *Two and Two Make Four*, c.1924.

OLD METHODS OF CALCULATING COSTS

W HEATH ROBINSON

270 'Old Methods of Calculating Costs',
from *Two and Two Make Four*, c.1924.

271 'The Clever Lad who Kept a Burroughs Calculator at School', from *Two and Two Make Four*, c.1924.

272 'Care Free Staff', from *Two and Two Make Four*, c.1924.

OLD · METHOD · OF · TOTALLING · CASH · SALES

273 'Old Method of Totalling Cash Sales',
from *Catching Runaway Pennies*, c.1922.

THE LAMSON PARAGON SUPPLY COMPANY

As was noted in the Introduction, Heath Robinson's earliest advertising commissions came from the Lamson Paragon Supply Company, which had been established in Ropemaker Street in the City of London in 1889 (figs 274–83). In 1893 they had moved into a large, newly built factory in Canning Town following the appointment of Robert Clark as manager. The company's main products were 'Check Books' that allowed shopkeepers to have detailed records of their sales, 'Plic Books' which provided carbon duplicates of correspondence, and paper bags.

Robert Clark, always progressive, was attracted to advertising as a means of promoting business, and had 'imported' from the United States Chas. Ed. Potter, an experienced advertising manager. It was Potter who, seeing a copy of *The Adventures of Uncle Lubin*, recognised that he had found the ideal artist to illustrate the advertising copy that he was writing. The regular meeting described in the Introduction resulted in a series of nine illustrated advertisements that were published in *The Grocer* between June and August 1903. They were then repeated.

By this time Potter had returned home. Robert Clark cabled Potter 'Send Substitute,' and the result was the arrival of another American, John Meath Evans, who having started as an advertising manager, was destined to become Managing Director of the Lamson Paragon organisation.

Evans and Heath Robinson soon settled into a comfortable working relationship, meeting regularly in his studio to work out ideas for the next few weeks' advertisements. Rough sketches were made in a 'Plic' book with Heath Robinson taking the top copy and Evans retaining the duplicate. The advertisements appeared in *The Grocer* during the remainder of 1903 and in 1904 were also published in the *Drapers' Record*.

In 1905 a full-page advertisement in *The Grocer* showed the two stands that Lamson Paragon had taken at the Grocers' Exhibition at the Agricultural Hall in London. The first of them showed the old way of making paper bags, by hand, and the newest machine making and printing 200 bags per minute.

"*Watch the bung-hole, but don't forget the spigot*"

THE PARAGON COUNTER CHECK BOOK SYSTEM looks after the spigot holes. Through its use you are able to keep a check on your stock; the cost of selling goods per each assistant; the price goods are sold at, etc.

PARAGON CHECK BOOKS prevent thoughtlessness, brings out the best in everybody, and gives your shop a good reputation for carefulness.

If this interests you, drop us a card so we may tell you more.

We make: Paper bags, more economical to use than wrapping paper, in lines especially adapted to *every* branch of business. *We make:* Check books for any and every known trade that employs assistants whose carefulness and industry it is desirable to insure.

You want right check books at right prices—then write us

Lamson Paragon Supply Co.
Limited

City Office: Works:
4, Queen St., Cheapside, E. C.   Canning Town, London, E.

View of Paragon Works, Canning Town, London, E. where Paragon productions are manufactured. Thrice round means a mile.

274 A half-page advertisement featuring an Uncle Lubin-like character published in *The Grocer*, 22 August 1903.

275 A page from a pocket book called *The Profits on Returns Book* issued by Lamson Paragon to promote its products, c.1895.

The Grocer reported that: 'The second stand was embellished with original drawings, which the company had prepared for advertising matter for the trade. This was a somewhat new departure, but the enterprise we fancy will be successful.' An accompanying photograph showed the second stand in the form of a shop front with large-scale drawings by Heath Robinson forming panels under the windows and other designs displayed in the windows.

In May 1904 Lamson Paragon had started to advertise in the *Stationery Trades Journal*, and in October 1905 that publication noted:

> A step recently taken indicates the gradually growing pressure which is being brought to bear to make their goods desired by the public. This is the commencement of mural advertising. The illustration which we give is a tiny reproduction of a design in colours on iron plate, which is now to be seen at the principal railway stations. The original character of the firm's advertisement has been noticeable for some time, and now that other forms of publicity are being adopted, handling their goods should become still more satisfactory.

The illustration referred to showed a winged messenger boy flying through the air to deliver Paragon ribbons and carbon paper to an eagerly waiting typist.

THE WORRIED MAN.

WHEN FOUND MAKE A NOTE OF

276 'The Worried Man', undated, pen, ink and blue crayon, 133 × 126 mm (5¼ × 5 in) (for a Lamson Paragon advertisement published in *The Grocer* on 13 October 1906 and repeated on 18 December 1909).

277 'When Found Make A Note Of', undated, pen and ink, 135 × 126 mm (5⅜ × 5 in) (for a Lamson Paragon advertisement).

OLIVER WANTS MORE

HE'S ASKING FOR MORE.

It's the old, old story.

It went on before Oliver Twist's time, and it's been going on ever since, and it will keep going on.

Is your assistant worth an increase?

Look over his sales, and see how much more he's selling than he did last year, or than his junior assistant.

If you don't know this, you ought to.

You don't pass an invoice for payment until you've checked it and examined the goods, do you? You want to know what you're getting for your money, don't you?

And yet you pay your assistant without knowing what you get in return.

It's not fair to you or him, is it?

Paragon Checks solve the difficulty.

It will only take a minute to write Dept. I for samples and prices, or if in town, call at our City Office, 4, Queen Street, E.C.

TO WORRIED MEN

TO those who worry, it's useless saying "Don't" or reciting platitudes, such as, "It's not work but worry that kills," etc.
What the worried man wants is a remedy—a remove-the-cause preventative.

Isn't that so, Worried Man?
Well, here's our little lot of advice:

For worrying about your cash—or forgetting to charge—or disputes with customers, etc., etc.,—PARAGON CHECK BOOKS.

For worrying about what you wrote last week—whether or not you ordered some goods you badly need now—PARAGON PLIC BOOKS AND PLIC POST-CARD BOOKS.

Thousands are using the above remedies and have quit worrying. You can go on, if you wish, but our advice is: "Don't; it doesn't pay and it ruins your health in the bargain."

Write to Dept. 3 for samples and prices, or if in town, call at our City Office and Salesroom, 4 St. Paul's Churchyard, E.C.

BIRMINGHAM OFFICE: 7A WARWICK PASSAGE

SOUTH AFRICA: 58 FLETCHER'S CHAMBERS DARLING STREET, CAPE TOWN

LAMSON PARAGON SUPPLY CO., L'T'D

Check Books, Plic Books, Paper Bags

CANNING TOWN, LONDON, E

LITTLE THINGS TELL IN EVERYTHING

SOME users of paper bags do not grasp the advertising opportunities a paper bag offers.

Often a phrase you use in your advertisements could be printed on your paper bags, and with the up-to-date type and good printing put on Paragon Paper Bags, combined with the fine qualities of the bags themselves, they should prove a strong, business-bringing, advertising medium.

You send the wording and we do the rest.

Samples and prices of Paragon Paper Bags for all trades on application to Department 1, or if in town, call at our City Office, 4, Queen Street, E.C.

278 Advertisement for Lamson Paragon 'Check Books' published in *The Drapers' Record*, 3 June 1905 and *The Grocer* in 1905.

279 Advertisement for Lamson Paragon 'Check Books' and 'Plic Books' published in *The Grocer*, 13 October 1906.

280 Advertisement for Lamson Paragon bags published in *The Drapers' Record*, 3 June 1905.

COME
AND SEE US

CHECK
BOOK
EXHIBIT
BAY 11
GROUND
FLOOR

WE will have two unique exhibits at the Grocers' Exhibition, Agricultural Hall, and we want you to call on us.

If you are dissatisfied with your present checking system, or if there is any weak point without sufficient protection, we hope you will not fail to mention it when you call. We can and will help you.

If you are not at present using check books, give us an opportunity of explaining their merits. We don't want you to buy anything you don't want, and we merely ask you to look into the matter.

PAPER BAG
EXHIBIT
ROW Z
EXHIBITS
No. 36
AND 38

If you want to see how Paragon Paper Bags give satisfaction to thousands of grocers, a visit to our Paper Bag Exhibit will be most entertaining and instructive. We will show you here a machine making and printing 200 paper bags a minute.

We want to see you all—those who know us and those who don't. We would specially like to meet those who have read our weekly chats on Paragon topics and up to the present time have not written us.

Lamson Paragon Supply Company, Lt'd

CHECK BOOKS, PAPER BAGS, PLIC BOOKS, GUMMED RECEIPT BOOKS
POST-CARD BOOKS AND DUPLICATING BOOKS FOR ALL PURPOSES

PARAGON WORKS, CANNING TOWN, LONDON, E

PARAGON PAPER BAGS FOR MILLINERY
AND ENVELOPES FOR GLOVES

PARAGON MILLINERY BAGS are of such good quality that they can justly be called the "aristocracy of paper bags."

Starting with reels of blank paper, the best the market affords, they pass through automatic bag-making machines, finishing with the printed bags ready for the customer. During the process every known means are used that will better the finished result. The printing on Paragon Millinery Bags is superior, and the type-designs exhibit the good taste which makes a Paragon Bag a bag Paragon.

There's nothing "loud" or "common" about Paragon Millinery Bags and they please the most fastidious shopkeeper and customer alike.

With all their merits they're not expensive.

PARAGON GLOVE ENVELOPES.—There is no neater, quicker, or better way of packing gloves, ribbons, laces, etc. than Paragon Glove Envelopes. They keep the gloves flat and prevent creasing. The envelope does not become ragged with handling as the case is with gloves wrapped in "nature brown." It takes just half the time to slip the gloves in the envelope than to wrap in ordinary paper.

Paragon Glove Envelopes are made in four delicate shades—Mauve, Primrose, Green, Blue—and are artistically printed in violet or black ink.

Quantities as low as 1000, assorted colours, if desired.

Samples and prices from Dept. 1.

Lamson Paragon Supply Company, Ltd.

PAPER BAGS, CHECK BOOKS, PLIC BOOKS, GUMMED RECEIPT BOOKS
POST-CARD BOOKS AND DUPLICATING BOOKS FOR ALL PURPOSES

PARAGON WORKS, CANNING TOWN, LONDON, E.

---

281 Full-page advertisement in *The Drapers' Record*, 16 September 1905.

282 Full-page advertisement in *The Grocer*, 9 September 1905.

283 Lamson Paragon
Christmas card 1905.

W. Heath Robinson's Published Drawings for Advertising

INTRODUCTION

What follows here is an attempt to list all of W. Heath Robinson's drawings and watercolours that were commissioned and published for advertising and publicity purposes. By its nature such material is ephemeral, and much of it was only circulated within narrow trade circles. There is no national archive for such material, as there is for books and periodicals, and many of the companies that originally commissioned the work have ceased trading or been absorbed into larger conglomerates. It is therefore inevitable that the listing is incomplete, and the author would welcome any additional information that readers can supply.

The items are listed here in alphabetical order of the company commissioning the work. The sizes given are page sizes, with height given first. 'Published' indicates an advertisement paid for by the manufacturer, 'Illustrated' a reproduction of an example of the work in a book or magazine. The following sources are referred to in abbreviated form:

W. Heath Robinson, *Get On With It*, G. Heath Robinson and J. Birch, London, n.d. (1920);

W. Heath Robinson, *My Line of Life*, Blackie & Son, London, 1938;

Quentin Robinson, *The Gentle Art of Advertising*, Duckworth, London, 1979.

THE PUBLISHED DRAWINGS

The Apollo Player and Piano Co. Ltd

1. 'Measuring customers for Apollo player pianos in the showroom of the Apollo Player and Piano Co. Ltd.'
A small line illustration
Published: *The Evening News*, 27 Jul 1923

Asbestos Cement Building Products

2. *The Making of Asbestos Cement Roofing as seen by W. Heath Robinson*, Asbestos Cement Building Products, Trafford Park, Manchester, n.d. [*c*.1930]
356 × 254 mm (14 × 10 in); 16 pp
Grey boards printed in black and blue, tied with a grey ribbon
Six full-page halftone illustrations
Illustrated: *My Line of Life*, facing p.178 (1); *The Gentle Art of Advertising*, pp 79–82 (4)

Ashby's Brewery

3. 'Mr Heath Robinson's dream after visiting Ashby's Brewery'
One full-page halftone illustration
Published: p.14 of an unidentified brewery publication

Barclay, Perkins & Co. Ltd

4. 'The Finest Thirst I Ever Knew – the thirst that saved a life'
Half-page press advertisement in line for Barclay's Lager
Published: *Punch*, 24 Jun 1925, p.xxv

5. 'It's Thirsty Work'
Full-page press advertisement in line for Barclay's Lager
Published: *Punch*, 7 Apr 1926, p.xxi

Barford & Perkins Ltd

6. 'The New Model Type WHY4 Roller'
Press advertisement in line, n.d.
Illustrated: *The Gentle Art of Advertising*, p.86

7. 'Smart Reverse Action by one of Barford & Perkins latest motor rollers to save the life of a chicken'
Illustration in red and black for the celluloid cover for a notebook, 1931
66 × 95 mm (2⅝ × 3¾ in)

Barnardo's Homes

8. 'To the Rescue'
A postcard, n.d.
Illustration in halftone

Bassetts Ltd

9. 'Greetings from Macadam', Christmas card, 1921
Four pages with two full-page drawings in two colours on the outside and a double-page line drawing inside
Note: The design was subsequently used for a Christmas card for Crow Catchpole & Co. Ltd.

Bayliss, Jones & Bayliss Ltd

10. Nibal Fencing and Wrought Iron Gates. Two line drawings for Bayliss, Jones & Bayliss Ltd, Wolverhampton, entitled:
a. 'The Making of "Bayliss Nibal" Railing'
b. 'How Wrought Iron Gates are Wrought'
Published:
a. *Punch Almanack* for 1933, p.xv
b. *Punch* Summer Number 1932, p.xv
Illustrated: Edgar Jones, *A History of GKN, Volume Two*, Macmillan, Houndmills and London, pp 223–5

Lewis Berger & Sons Ltd

11. 'Lewis Berger of the House of Berger, his paint'

A small line illustration

Published: *The Evening News*, 27 July 1923

John Booth & Sons

12. *Problems of a Structural Engineer* by W. Heath Robinson, with a foreword by Ashley Sterne. John Booth & Sons, Bolton, Lancashire, n.d. (*c*.1930)

290 × 201 mm (11⅜ × 7⅞ in); 24 pp

Pictorial brown wrappers

Seven full-page halftone illustrations and eight smaller drawings in line

13. *Booth Steelwork,* John Booth & Sons, Hulton Steel Works, Bolton. n.d. (*c*.1937)

280 × 215 mm (11 × 8½ in); 66 pp

Blue wrappers

Seven full-page halftone illustrations, of which four are reprinted from the previous publication

Boulton & Paul Ltd

14. Press advertisement in line for Boulton & Paul poultry houses

Published: *Illustrated London News*, 10 Jun 1933, p.858

Bovis Ltd.

15. 'Bovisms'. Bovis Ltd, Contractors & Decorators, Upper Berkeley Street, London, W1, n.d., [1919]

280 × 205 mm (11 × 8 in)

A dark pink paper portfolio containing 17 printed sheets with nine full-page illustrations, of which two are by Heath Robinson, both in line, one in red and black

Note: Other artists are Lawson Wood, H.M. Bateman, Peter Fraser, Geo. Morrow, Bert Thomas, Alfred Leete and Reginald Arkell.

Burberrys Ltd

16. 'Burberrys New Year's Slogan: Quality – Individual and Personal Attention'

Quarter-page press advertisement in line

Published: *The Evening Standard*, 1 Jan 1940, p.12

Illustrated: *The Gentle Art of Advertising*, p.73

Burroughs Adding Machine Company

17. *Catching Runaway Pennies*, Burroughs Adding Machine Company, London, 1922

275 × 215 mm (10⅞ × 8½ in); 8 pp

An advertising leaflet with one line drawing on the back page

18. *Two and Two Make Four*, Burroughs Adding Machine Ltd, London, n.d. [*c*.1924]

223 × 144 mm (8¾ × 5⅝ in); 20 pp

Brown card covers with line drawings front and rear

Ten half-page drawings in line (including covers)

Note: The drawings were originally made for monthly Calendar Blotters in 1922.

Canadian Pacific

19. *The Story of Cocktails* as pictured by W. Heath Robinson and described by Anthony Armstrong. Reprinted from *The Strand Magazine*. Canadian Pacific, London, 1932

186 × 244 mm (7⅜ × 9⅝ in); 16 pp

Wrappers printed in black and orange

Ten half-page illustrations and seven circular vignettes in orange and black halftone, with a photograph of Heath Robinson painting one of them that is not reproduced in *The Strand Magazine*

20. *Cocktail Mixing* shaken up by W. Heath Robinson. Canadian Pacific, London, n.d. (1938)

145 × 141 mm (5¾ × 5½ in); 12 pp (inc wrappers)

Pictorial wrappers printed in orange and black

Four full-page, five half-page and six circular vignette illustrations in orange and black halftone

City Dairy Co. Ltd

21. *We Testify of That We Do Know*, City Dairy Co. Ltd, Toronto Canada, n.d. (1903)

172 × 123 mm (6¾ × 4⅞ in); [16 pp]

Brown wrappers with a pictorial design by WHR printed in black, red, blue and white

Clarkhill Automatic Water Heaters Ltd

22. 'This is a complicated way to obtain hot water, but . . .', Clarkhills Ltd., n.d. (*c*.1926)

204 × 125 mm (8 × 4⅞ in)

A six-page promotional brochure in card covers

One halftone illustration to the front in red and black

Illustrated: *Commercial Art*, Mar 1927, vol.II, p.115

Colman's Mustard

23. 'The only village in England that did not join the Mustard Club'

Full-page press advertisement with a half-page drawing in line

Published: *Punch*, 1 Feb 1928, p.x

Connolly Bros (Curriers) Ltd

24. *Nothing Like Leather* by W. Heath Robinson, Connolly Bros (Curriers) Ltd, London, n.d. (1920)

217 × 139 mm (8½ × 5½ in); 12 pp

Cream card covers decorated with silhouettes

Six full-page and three smaller line drawings

Illustrated: Percy V. Bradshaw, *Art in Advertising*, The Press Art School, London, 1925, p.329 (1)

25. 'Connolly Bros Motor Hides'

Full-page press advertisement in line featuring the four silhouettes from the cover of *Nothing Like Leather*

Published: W. Heath Robinson, *The Home Made Car*, Duckworth, London, n.d. (1921), p.15

26. *Light on Leather* shed by W. Heath Robinson, Connolly Bros. (Curriers) Ltd, London, n.d. (1922)

217 × 139 mm (8½ × 5½ in); 24 pp

Cream card covers with pictorial design in red and black

Six full-page and 17 smaller illustrations

Illustrated: Percy V. Bradshaw, *Art in Advertising*, The Press Art School, London, 1925, p.329 (1)

27. *Tough Testimonials*, Connolly Bros (Curriers) Ltd, London, n.d. (1924)

217 × 139 mm (8½ × 5½ in); 32 pp

Cream card covers with a design by H.M. Bateman in red and black

Numerous illustrations by H.M. Bateman, R. Bull, F. Heubner, A. Leete, W. Heath Robinson, H. Rountree, J. Routier, W. Sluiter, L. Tayler and A. Watts, of which four line drawings are by W. Heath Robinson

28. *Nothing Takes the Place of Leather* by W. Heath Robinson, Connolly Bros (Curriers) Ltd, London, n.d. (1925)

139 × 217 mm (5½ × 8½ in); 20 pp

Cream card covers with a pictorial design in red and black. Six full-page and 17 smaller line drawings

29. *Leather Breeding on the Wandle* described by W. Heath Robinson, Connolly Bros (Curriers) Ltd, n.d. (1927)

139 × 217 mm (5½ × 8½ in); 20 pp

Cream card covers with a pictorial design in brown and black

Six full-page and 14 smaller line drawings

30. *Cattle Culture at Connolly's Leather College on the Wandle*, described by W. Heath Robinson, Connolly Bros (Curriers) Ltd, London, n.d. (1930)

139 × 217 mm (5½ × 8½ in); 20 pp

Cream card covers with a pictorial design in green and black

Six full-page and 14 smaller line drawings

31. *Leather For Ever* by W. Heath Robinson, Connolly Bros (Curriers) Ltd, London, n.d. (1931)

217 × 139 mm (8½ × 5½ in); 20 pp

Red and cream card covers with a pictorial design in black

Six full-page and 14 smaller line drawings

32. *Heath Robinson on Leather* (Collected Edition), Connolly Bros (Curriers) Ltd, London, n.d. (1932)

312 × 250 mm (12¼ × 9⅞ in); 48 pp

Brown leather-grained card covers with a pictorial design in black

22 half-page, 82 smaller and six vignette line drawings

Note: All of the illustrations appeared in earlier Connolly booklets.

33. *Connolly Chronicles* retold by W. Heath Robinson, Connolly Bros (Curriers) Ltd, London, n.d. (1933)

272 × 194 mm (10¾ × 7⅝ in); 20 pp

Grey card covers printed in black and white with a pictorial design

Six full-page and 17 smaller illustrations

34. *Connolly-Land* by W. Heath Robinson, Connolly Bros (Curriers) Ltd, London, n.d. (1934)

258 × 134 mm (10⅛ × 5¼ in); 14 pp + fold-out plan

Grained beige card covers with a pictorial design in black

Five full-page and nine smaller line drawings, plus a triple-page full-colour fold-out plan

35. *The Business Man's Encyclopedia Connollyca*, compiled by W. Heath Robinson, Connolly Bros (Curriers) Ltd, London, n.d. (1935)

258 × 134 mm (10⅛ × 5¼ in); 20 pp

Cream and red grained card cover with a pictorial design in black

36 half-page or smaller line drawings

36. *Connolly Customers* as imagined by W. Heath Robinson, Connolly Bros (Curriers) Ltd, London, n.d. (1936)

152 × 231 mm (6 × 9 in); 20 pp

White card covers with a pictorial design in blue and black

Six full-page and 14 smaller line drawings

37. *Heath Robinson on Leather* (Collected Edition). Connolly Bros (Curriers) Ltd, London, n.d. (1938)

312 × 250 mm (12¼ × 9⅞ in); 48 pp

Grey leather-grained card covers with four silhouettes in black

Six full-page, 22 half-page, 77 smaller and six vignette line drawings

Note: This is a revised version of the 1932 collection with six full-page drawings from *Connolly Chronicles* added.

38. *I Can't Improve on That Mr Connolly*. The story of Connolly leather's first hundred years 1878–1978. Connolly Bros (Curriers) Ltd, London, 1978

310 × 250 mm (12¼ × 9⅞ in); 64 pp

Brown leather-grained card covers with a full-colour pictorial design

Numerous photographs and a reprint of *Heath Robinson on Leather*, 1932

39. *Connolly Calendar*, 1989, Connolly Bros (Curriers) Ltd, Wimbledon, 1988

Limited edition of 1000 copies signed by Oliver Robinson and Tim Connolly

485 × 380 mm (19 × 15 in); 14 spiral-bound leaves

Pictorial card envelope printed in cream, orange, grey and black

13 line drawings, one of which is repeated on the cover, taken from *Light on Leather* and *Leather for Ever*. Printed on grained paper

40. *Connolly Calendar*, 1990, Connolly Bros (Curriers) Ltd, Wimbledon, 1989

Limited edition of 1000 copies signed by Oliver Robinson and Tim Connolly

380 × 478 mm (15 × 18⅞ in); 14 spiral-bound leaves

Pictorial card envelope printed in black and grey

Full-colour cover design of *Connolly-Land*, and 14 line drawings from *Leather Breeding on the Wandle* and *Cattle Culture*

41. *Connolly Calendar*, 1991, Connolly Bros (Curriers) Ltd, Wimbledon, 1990

Limited edition of 1000 copies signed by Alan B. Robinson and Tim Connolly

477 × 382 mm (18¾ × 15 in); 14 spiral-bound leaves

Pictorial card envelope printed in cream, grey and black

21 line drawings reproduced from *Connolly Chronicles*

Continental Tyre Company

42. Continental Tyre Company, Germany

Two (or more?) full-page halftone cartoons in red and blue featuring 'Continental Ballon'

Published: *Echo-Continental*, the company house magazine in Germany. n.d. (c.1927)

43. 'The Evolution of the Continental Tyre'

A set of eight postcards with halftone illustrations in red and black, 1928

a. A prehistoric effort to reduce road-shocks

b. Self-starters and shock-absorbers at the annual hill-climb under the patronage of the Sphinx

c. Filling a 'Middle-Age' tyre during a rough passage of the royal family

d. Demonstrates the resiliency and smooth running of the Continental Balloon irrespective of roads and loads

e. With the Continental Giant Pneumatic you are 'at home' on the road at all times

f. Illustrates the reason why Continental Balloon Tyres 'always stand the test'

g. Giant Pneumatics add another 'storey' to the development of the motor omnibus

h. The last word in comfort and safety on the road

William Cook & Co. Ltd

44. Prospectus of William Cook & Co. Ltd, Sheffield, n.d.

Size and format unknown

Binding unknown

Six full-page halftone illustrations

Illustrated: *The Gentle Art of Advertising*, pp 52–7

Co-operative-Permanent Building Society

45. 'A Good Resolution'

Quarter-page press advertisement in line for Co-operative-Permanent Building Society, London

Published: *The Evening Standard*, 1 Jan 1934, p.16

Illustrated: *The Gentle Art of Advertising*, p.76

Robert Cort & Sons Ltd

46. *This Coke Business*. Robert Cort and Sons Ltd, Reading, n.d. (1922)

219 × 214 mm (8⅝ × 8⅜ in)

Pictorial cover design by W. Heath Robinson printed in brown and black, no other illustrations

Illustrated: *The Gentle Art of Advertising*, p.88

Courtaulds Ltd

47. 'A New Year's Resolution – To Make Certain that Your Shirts and Pyjamas bear the Registered LUVISCA Tab'

Quarter-page press advertisement in line

Published: *The Evening Standard*, 1 Jan 1934, p.16

Illustrated: *The Gentle Art of Advertising*, p.75

William Crawford & Sons Ltd

48. *Mr. Heath Robinson's Conception of a Modern Biscuit Plant*

Full-page coloured press advertisement for William Crawford & Sons Ltd, Edinburgh, Liverpool and London

Published: *Punch* (Almanac Number), 6 Nov 1933

Also printed as a card insert for tins of biscuits

The 'Cropwell' Herd

49. [Calendar for 1923]

Two line drawings for a calendar advertising Cuthbert C. Smith's 'Cropwell' herd of middle-white pigs in Nottinghamshire

[Published version not seen]

Curzon Bros, Ltd

50. 'Curzon Bros. coupon delivering machine to meet the great response to their magnificent offer'

A small line illustration

Published: *The Evening News*, 27 Jul 1923

The Daimler Company Ltd

51. *The Daimler Way Of Ensuring Quality Control*, The Daimler Company Ltd, Coventry, 1920

Size and format unknown

Binding unknown

Four full-page line drawings

Illustrated: *Commercial Art*, Jun 1927, vol.II, p.257 (1)

The Direct Supply Aerated Water Co. Ltd

52. 'A Seasonable Resolution – Make sure of a direct supply of refreshing drinks throughout the coming year'

Quarter-page press advertisement in line

Published: *The Evening Standard*, 1 Jan 1934, p.17

A. Duckham & Co Ltd

53. *Technical Talks*, A Duckham & Co. Ltd, London, n.d., [1925]

Six full-page halftone illustrations

215 × 138 mm (8½ × 5⅜ in); 32 pp

Blue card covers

G. & T. Earle [1925] Ltd

54. *The Wonders of Wilmington*, depicted by W. Heath Robinson, G. & T. Earle [1925] Ltd, Wilmington, Hull, n.d. (1927)

270 × 403 mm (10⅝ × 15⅞ in); 12 pp

Pictorial leather-grained boards printed in black

Five full-page halftone illustrations

55. A set of five postcards reproducing the above illustrations, issued in a printed envelope

56. The drawings also used in press advertisements in *The Contract Journal*, Feb 1927

57. *Earle's Early Etchings*, G. & T. Earle Ltd, Hull, 1949

175 × 267 mm (6⅞ × 10½ in); 12 pp

Pictorial wrappers with a photograph of Hope Works and Quarry

Five full-page halftone illustrations

Reprinted in pale blue card covers by Blue Circle Industries Inc., 1984

Note: The illustrations are reprinted from *The Wonders of Wilmington*.

J.C. Eno Ltd

58. 'The Buoyancy of Good Health'

Full-page halftone press advertisement for Eno's fruit salts

Published: *Get On With It*, n.d. (1920)

Ever-Ready Razor Products Ltd

59. 'A Good New Year's Resolution – Be EVER READY in an Emergency'

Quarter-page press advertisement in line

Published: *The Evening Standard*, 1 Jan 1934, p.17

Firth Brothers

60. 'Furniture in the Making', a series of small line drawings in a single frame for a press advertisement

Published: *The Weekly Herald*, 5 Nov 1937

Two of the drawings were extracted and used in a promotional brochure

Note: *The Weekly Herald* was a local paper published in the North London boroughs of Tottenham and Edmonton.

61. 'Some Interesting Pianos Not Made by Firth Brothers', a series of small line drawings in a single frame for a press advertisement

Published: *The Weekly Herald*, 25 Nov 1938

Fletcher, Burrows & Co. Ltd

62. The *'First' Colliery*, an almanac of four drawings by W. Heath Robinson, With the Compliments of Fletcher, Burrows & Co. Ltd., Atherton, Lancashire, 1922

548 × 358 mm (21⅝ × 14 in)

Five cream card leaves joined with a green silk cord passing through brass-reinforced holes

Four mounted halftone plates and a cover drawing in line

Note: The calendar is unusual in running from Apr 1922 to Mar 1923. The calendar was reissued by Lancashire Associated Collieries in 1938.

63. A set of four postcards using the same designs were issued by Manchester Collieries Ltd, 28 Cross St, Manchester

The Florists' Telegraph Delivery Service

64. 'Say It With Flowers', a single-sheet leaflet with a line drawing to the front and promotional copy to the verso

217 × 140 mm (8½ × 5½ in)

Thomas Forman & Sons

65. 'Brain Waves' and 'To Save Trouble', two sets of 6 full-colour drawings to be used in tailor-made calendars for small businesses

Each image finely lithographed on a separate sheet of cream card with 'Brain Waves' or 'To Save Trouble' embossed at the top and the client's name and a date block printed below. The sheets joined with a tasselled green cord at the top

Note: These pictures were re-issued as greetings cards by Camden Graphics in 1982.

66. Postcards using coloured images from *The Monarchs of Merry England* (1907) with text advertising various small traders on the verso

General Electric Co. Ltd

67. 'Osram Valves a Tonic to Any Set'

Two press advertisements in line

Published: *Printer's Pie*, 1934, p.8; unidentified newspapers

Illustrated: Chris Beetles Ltd exhibition catalogue, London, Mar 1987 (1)

Goodall, Backhouse & Co.

68. 'How we make sure there are 2,400 drops of flavour in every 9d bottle of Yorkshire Relish'

Full-colour design for show-card and postcard, n.d. [1923]

Listed: *Stanley Gibbons Postcard Catalogue*, 1981

Luis Gordon & Sons Ltd

69. 'Impressions of a Well Known Sherry Works by W. Heath Robinson'

Coloured display card for Domecq's sherry

Illustrated: *The Gentle Art of Advertising*, p.77

Note: Made with the headings 'Domecq's Sherry' and 'Domecq's Magnola Sherry'.

Great Northern Laundry

70. 'Laundry Impressions' – a series of postcard designs

Drawings in line and tone, printed in black and ochre, 1923

a. No.1. The collection calls

b. No.2. Up-to-date plant in the wash house

Note: There are probably others in the series.

The Great Western Railway

71. *Railway Ribaldry* being 96 pages of railway humour by W. Heath Robinson, The Great Western Railway, Paddington Station, 1935

247 × 186 mm (9¾ × 7⅜ in); 96 pp

Pictorial card wrappers printed in green, yellow and black

45 full-page drawings and 52 vignettes in line

Note: a few copies were bound up in paper-covered boards for presentation to shareholders.

The Gre-Solvent Company

72. 'How Dad Inadvertently Brought Home the Gre-Solvent'

A full-colour press advertisement

Published: *A Day in the Home of Ease*, 1924

73. *The Tale Of A Great Discovery*, The Gre-Solvent Company, Leeds, n.d. (1929)

125 × 175 mm (4⅞ × 6⅞ in); 8 pp

Printed throughout on coarse yellow-brown paper

11 line drawings, one of which is repeated on the front, derived from the earlier press advertisement

W.P. Hartley

74. [A new method of manufacturing marmalade]

A page of six line drawings advertising Hartley's Marmalade

Published: *Printer's Pie*, 1925, p.v

Illustrated: *Meals on Wheels*, Souvenir Press, London, 1989, p.10

Hazelbourne Laundry

75. 'As Others See Us', Hazelbourne Laundry, Balham, London, n.d.

Date and size unknown

Four-sheet fold-out leaflet on cream paper

Seven line drawings

Hercules Cycle and Motor Company Ltd

76. 'A Perfect Picnic on the Week-End All-Weather Tandem'

A full colour press advertisement for Hercules bicycles

Published: *Hercules Cycle Magazine*, n.d. (1935)

High Duty Alloys Ltd

77. 'The War in the Air' by W. Heath Robinson. A series of full-page halftone press advertisements for High Duty Alloys Ltd., Slough:

No.1. BLIND FLYING is flying when you can't exactly see where you are going – this is how young pilots are trained to do it
Published: *Flight*, 11 Sep 1941, p.advt.viii

No.2. AERO CAMOUFLAGE, a wartime expedient to make a plane indistinguishable from its background
Published: *The Aeroplane*, 12 Sep 1941, p.advt.15

No.3. TO BALE OUT is to leave the plane at a moment's notice when your services are required elsewhere
Published: *Flight*, 13 Nov 1941, p.advt.27

No.4. THE CRATE an old fashioned but useful type of machine not yet adapted to wartime requirements
Published: *Flight*, 25 Dec 1941, p.advt.vii

No.5. THE CEILING is the highest point in the stratosphere at which the crew can carry on, and this is how they know when they get there
Published: *Flight*, 5 Feb 1942, p.advt.25

No.6. 1942 MODEL. A new type especially designed to confuse the enemy by firing in all directions at the same time
Published: *Flight*, 19 Mar 1942, p.advt.23

No.7. PARACHUTE LANDING. This is the improved method providing every comfort for the parachutist
Published: *Flight*, 30 Apr 1942, facing p.440. Repeated 30 Jul 1942

No.8. MANOEUVRABILITY is the power to turn round quickly and dodge the snags in the line of flight
Published: *Flight*, 11 Jun 1942, p.advt.19

Note: It is probable that all of these drawings were published in both *Flight* and *The Aeroplane*, with the exception of no.2 which does not seem to have appeared in *Flight*.

Horrockses, Crewdson & Co. Ltd

78. *How It Is Done! The manufacture of cotton fabrics according to Heath Robinson – the famous humorist*, Horrockses, Crewdson & Co. Ltd, Manchester, 1921

260 × 210 mm (10¼ × 8¼ in)

16 pp front matter, 104 pp diary interleaved with blotting paper

Brown Morocco-grained cloth with a coloured pictorial onlay

Three full-page halftone illustrations

Hovis Ltd

79. *An Unconventional History of Hovis*. Pictured by W. Heath Robinson. Recounted by S.C. Peacock. Hovis Ltd, Macclesfield, n.d. (1926)

247 × 188 mm (9¾ × 7⅜ in); 24 pp

Blue wrappers titled in black and tied at the spine with blue cord

Ten full-page halftone illustrations

80. 'W. Heath Robinson on Hovis'

Full-page, full-colour press advertisement for Hovis Ltd. A coloured version of the last illustration in the above booklet

Published: *The Sketch* Christmas Number 1926, p.1; *Punch Almanack* for 1927, 1 Nov 1926; *Nash's Pall Mall Magazine*, Jan 1927, back cover

Note: This image was issued by Hovis as a poster in 1973.

Inecto

81. Press advertisement for Inecto hair restorer, 1925

International Stores

82. 'Delicate Apparatus for Testing Cylindo Aroma'

Press advertisement in line for Cylindo Tea

Published: *Cambridge Daily News*, 8 Oct 1936, p.6 and 5 Nov 1936, p.2

83. 'Something Worth Having'

Press advertisement in line for International Stores' cakes and biscuits

Published: *Cambridge Daily News*, 22 Oct 1936, p.4

Kado Carbon Papers

84. 'An Instructive Afternoon at the Kado Works'

Press advertisement in line

Published: *The Official Guide to Holborn*, fifth edition, J. Burrow, London, 1937, p.9

Also used on the company's technical data sheets

Kensitas

85. 'Kind to All Throats, Whipsnade, 1931'

Press advertisement in line for Kensitas cigarettes

Note: It is not known whether this was published, but a rough drawing for it was sold at Sotheby's in Oct 1989.

86. 'No thanks, I'd rather have a Kensitas'

Full-page press advertisement

Published: *Punch*, 12 Jun 1935

T. Kerfoot & Co.

87. 'The Manufacture and Testing of Mineral Spring Granules'

Four-panel press advertisement in line for T. Kerfoot & Co., Bardsley, Lancs

Published: Spring 1922(?)

Lamson Paragon Supply Company

88. Numerous press advertisements mainly in line, for Lamson Paragon Supply Company, 4 Queen St, Cheapside, London, advertising paper bags, check books, 'plic' books and other related products

Published in *The Grocer*, *The Drapers' Record* and other trade magazines between Apr 1903 and 1907

89. Press advertisements, mainly in line, for Lamson Paragon Company, 4 Queen St, Cheapside, London, advertising M. & M. Paragon Typewriter ribbons and Paragon carbon paper

Published in *Stationery Trades Journal*, *Pitman's Phonetic Journal* and other trade magazines in 1904–5

Allen Lane

90. 'Mr W. Heath Robinson's Idea of a Busy Afternoon in a Publisher's Office'

Christmas card, n.d. (*c*.1933)

Illustrated: *The Private Library*, vol.7, no.3, Autumn 1984, p.132; *The Gentle Art of Advertising*, endpapers (modified)

R.J. Lea Ltd

91. 'The Twelve Virtues of Chairman', R.J, Lea Ltd, Manchester, 1915–16

A series of 12 full-page halftone press advertisements for Chairman tobacco:

No.1. 'Attractive aroma'.
Published: *Punch*, 14 Jul 1915, p.v; *London Opinion*, 25 Sep 1915, vol.46, p.466

No.2. 'A solace to the very end'
Published: *Punch*, 11 Aug 1915, p.vii

No.3. 'Entire absence of burning sensation'
Published: *Punch*, 8 Sep 1915, p.vii; *London Opinion*, 16 Oct 1915, vol.47, p.101

No.4. 'Fragrance which all enjoy'
Published: *Punch*, 20 Oct 1915, p.ix; *London Opinion*, 6 Nov 1915, vol.47, p.245

No.5. 'Its soothing properties'
Published: *Punch*, 10 Nov 1915, p.ix; *London Opinion*, 27 Nov 1915, vol.47, p.385

No.6. 'Promotes geniality'
Published: *Punch*, 8 Dec 1915, p.ix; *London Opinion*, 8 Jan 1916, vol.48, p.61

No.7. 'It steadies the nerves'
Published: *Punch*, 12 Jan 1916, p.ix; *London Opinion*, 29 Jan, 1916, vol.48, p.184

No.8. 'Its taking qualities'
Published: *Punch*, 9 Feb 1916, p.ix; *London Opinion*, 19 Feb 1916, vol.48, p.300

No.9. 'Banishes discomfort and brings content'
Published: *Punch*, 8 Mar 1916, p.ix; *London Opinion*, 11 Mar 1916, vol.48, p.413

No.10. 'It suits most palates'
Published: *Punch*, 12 Apr 1916, p.ix

No.11. 'It promotes Mark Tapleyism'
Published: *Punch*, 10 May 1916, p.ix

No.12. 'It is an economy'
Published: *Punch*, 14 Jun 1916, p.ix

92. 'A Chairman Calamity'

Full-page halftone press advertisement for Chairman Tobacco

Published: *London Opinion* Christmas Extra, 1915, p.68; *Punch Almanack* for 1916 (pages unnumbered)

Lever Bros Ltd

93. 'Heath Robinson's Idea of Comfort'

Press advertisement in line for Lever Bros 'Comfort' soap

Published: *The Humorist*, 10 May 1924, p.388

Illustrated: *Commercial Art*, Jun 1927, vol.II, p.256

Note: This drawing was also included in a portfolio of 12 drawings by different artists advertising Comfort soap.

Limmer & Trinidad Lake Asphalt Co. Ltd

94. Full-colour drawing for use at a trade exhibition, Nov 1921

2,000 prints of the picture were made for publicity purposes

F. Lyons & Co. Ltd

95. 'A new machine for the mass production of Swiss Rolls'

A press advertisement in line

Publication not seen

Macdonald, Greenlees & Williams (Distillers) Ltd

96. 'Sandy Macdonald's Scotch Whisky'

Full-page, full-colour press advertisement

Published: *The Sketch* Christmas Number 1922, p.36

John Mackintosh & Sons Ltd

97. 'W. Heath Robinson's Impression of Toffee Town'

Full-page press advertisement in line for J. Mackintosh & Sons Ltd, Nottingham, advertising Toffee de Luxe

Published: *Daily Mail*, 1 Oct 1921, front page; *The Sphere*, 22 Oct 1921, p.viii; *The Passing Show*, 5 Nov 1921; *Punch*, 16 Nov 1921, p.vii

Note: The drawing was also included in a promotional booklet published by Mackintosh.

98. 'Mackintosh's Toffee de Luxe is reduced to 8d per quarter – Heath Robinson's idea of how the news will be announced'

Press advertisement in line, 127 × 102 mm (5 × 4 in)

Published: *Daily Mail*, 1 Dec 1921, p.14

99. 'Mackintosh's call in the aid of Mr W. Heath Robinson to help Santa Claus deliver Toffee de Luxe on Christmas Eve'

Full-page press advertisement in line

Published: *Daily Mail*, 23 Dec 1922, front page

Manchester Cotton Bleachers and Finishers

100. 'Some Interesting Processes in an Up-to-date Bleach Works'

Full-page press advertisement in line

Published: *The Manchester Guardian Commercial*, 30 Jun 1927

Note: This advertisement was paid for by 21 companies in the region, listed at the foot of the advert.

Mazda

101. [Mazda light bulbs]

Design for a showcard in 1921

Meccano Ltd

102. 'Meccanotes'

One full-page halftone illustration and three small line drawings

Published: *Get On With It*, 1920, pp 50–51; *Meccano Magazine*, 1933

J. Millhoff & Co. Ltd

103. 'More Unsolicited Testimonials'

A full-page halftone illustration

Published: *Get On With It*, 1920, p.36

104. 'Applause', a booklet of celebrity testimonials for De Reszke cigarettes. Includes on pp 8–9 four drawings in pen and wash by WHR. n.d. [1921]

Note: The drawings are taken from 'More Unsolicited Testimonials' above.

105. 'Luxurious facilities provided at well-known cigarette store for selecting without prejudice the most congenial brand'

A small line illustration

Published: *The Evening News*, 27 July 1923

Moss Bros & Co. Ltd

106. *Behind The Scenes at Moss Bros with Heath Robinson*, Moss Bros & Co. Ltd, Covent Garden, London, n.d. (1936).

218 × 295 mm (8⅝ × 11⅝ in); 16 pp

Pictorial card covers printed in orange and black

15 full-page halftone illustrations

Illustrated: *The Gentle Art of Advertising*, pp 32–45

Nabisco

107. 'How they cope with the New Year's demand for Shredded Wheat'

Quarter-page press advertisement in line

Published: *Evening Standard*, 1 Jan 1940, p.13

Illustrated: *The Gentle Art of Advertising*, p.74

James Neill & Co. (Sheffield) Ltd

108. Eclipse Razors

Seven small line drawings on one page

Published: *Punch* Spring Number, 1940

Newton, Chambers & Co. Ltd

109. *Thorncliffe Visited* by W. Heath Robinson, Newton, Chambers & Co. Ltd, Thorncliffe, Near Sheffield, n.d. [1924]

205 × 137 mm (8⅛ × 5⅜ in); 16 pp

Pictorial card wrappers

Seven full-page and two smaller drawings in line

110. *How Izal is Made. Solid facts made light* by W. Heath Robinson, Newton, Chambers & Co. Ltd, Thorncliffe, n.d.

Size unknown; 16 pp

Note: This is a variant of *Thorncliffe Visited*, using the same drawings.

111. 'Izal Kills Germs'. 10 postcards by W. Heath Robinson. Newton, Chambers & Co Ltd, Thorncliffe, n.d.

A set of 10 postcards, illustrated in line, in a brown pictorial envelope

Note: Four of the cards appear to have been drawn in the early 1920s whilst the other six are in a later 1930s style. The envelope design was used on the cover of *Thorncliffe Visited*.

112. 'Duroid'. A set of 11 drawings in line advertising 'Duroid' road surfacing. n.d. [1930s]

262 × 130 mm (10⅜ × 5⅛ in); 11 leaves

Note: These were originally issued on blotters sent to local council employees. A small number of sets of proofs were issued in plain black paper folders. The drawings were later reissued printed on pale blue card.

The Nithsdale Silver Fox Ranch

113. *The Silver Fox Argosy*, The Nithsdale Silver Fox Ranch, Thornhill, Dumfries, 1934

320 × 230 mm (12⅝ × 9 in); [72 pp]

Art vellum boards titled in black

Numerous illustrations, of which one full-page and one smaller line drawing are by WHR

114. 'How Mr. Heath Robinson thinks Nithsdale Silver Foxes are fed'

Full-page halftone press advertisement

Published: *Fur Farming*, vol. 8, no.4, Nov 1932

Norris, Henty & Gardners Ltd

115. A series of illustrated blotters with monthly calendars. Printed in black and white on thin card with pink blotting paper bonded to the verso. n.d. (*c*.1922)

120 × 188 mm (4¾ × 7⅜ in)

The North Eastern Marine Engineering Co. Ltd

116. 'An early attempt at superheating'

A halftone design for a postcard. n.d.

Nugget Polish Co.

117. 'Resolve to put your best foot forward – use Nugget boot polish and step brightly through 1934'

Quarter-page press advertisement in line

Published: *The Evening Standard*, 1 Jan 1934, p.16

118. 'Demonstrating the degree of distinction to be acquired by all users of Nugget'

Quarter-page press advertisement in line for Nugget boot polish

Published: *The Evening Standard*, 1 Jan 1937, p.23

119. 'Use Nugget boot polish and brighten your outlook on life'

Quarter-page press advertisement in line

Published: *The Evening Standard*, 2 Jan 1939, p.17

120. 'Begin the New Year well by joining the long chain of users of Nugget boot polish'

Quarter-page press advertisement in line

Published: *The Evening Standard*, 1 Jan 1940, p.12

Illustrated: *The Gentle Art of Advertising*, p.72

Oppenheimer's

121. 'The Episodes of Ebenezer Phizzletop', Oppenheimer's, pipe makers of 38 Finsbury Square, E.C.2. London, n.d.

143 × 90 mm (5⅝ × 3½ in); 32 pp

Buff pictorial wrappers

10 full-page line drawings

Oxo Ltd

122. Oxo press advertisement and/or showcard, 1922

There are surviving letters to WHR from Oxo discussing this, but no published examples have been seen. The drawing featured a billiard room with two white balls and the rest forming the word OXO, called 'The Oxo Break'

123. 'An idea for Producing More Oxo to Meet Wartime Needs'

A full-page halftone magazine advertisement in black and white

Published: *My Home*, Nov 1941

A. & F. Pears Ltd

124. 'The Unruffled Air'

Double-page, halftone illustration advertising Pears' Solid Brilliantine

Published: *Get On With It*, 1920, pp 28–9

Peek Frean & Co.

125. 'The Heath Robinson Golf Course – Packed with Peek Frean's Biscuits'

Full-colour biscuit tin, n.d. [*c*.1925]

273 × 180 × 45 mm (10¾ × 7⅛ × 1¾ in)

As well as biscuits, the tin contained a golf game. There was a shop display card promoting the tin

Illustrated: Chris Beetles Ltd exhibition catalogue, London, 2002 (original watercolour)

Philips Glowlamp Works Ltd

126. *The Wireless Adventures of Mr. Pimple*, with compliments of Philips Glowlamp Works Ltd, 1924

250 × 165 mm (9⅞ × 6½ in); 16 pp

Cream card wrappers with a pictorial design in line

Six full-page line drawings and six vignettes

Note: This booklet was also published with the text written in Dutch.

The Port of Manchester Warehouses Ltd

127. *Then and Now* illustrated by W. Heath Robinson, The Port of Manchester Warehouses Limited, Trafford Park, Manchester, 1921

283 × 219 mm (11⅛ × 8⅝ in); 48 pp

Brown paper wrappers with a pictorial design in black and yellow

Six full-page halftone illustrations and 16 smaller line drawings

Illustrated: *The Gentle Art of Advertising*, pp 46–51 (6); *Commercial Art*, Jun 1927, vol.II, p.258 (1)

Hector Powe

128. 'The History of a Pair of Trousers'

A full-page press advertisement in line for Hector Powe, Tailors, London

Published: *Pow-Wow*, the house magazine for Hector Powe, *c*.1924

Reference: Percy V. Bradshaw, *Art in Advertising*, The Press Art School, London, 1925, p.158. Bradshaw refers to two other WHR drawings, but these have not been seen.

129. 'Heath Robinson's Idea of Hector Powe Service'

A full page drawing in line

Published: *Pow Wow*, 1932

The Practical Etching Service Ltd

130. *The Gentle Art of Reproducing*, W. Heath Robinson, Comments by A. P. Garland. The Practical Etching Service Ltd., London. n.d. (1931)

285 × 215 mm (11¼ × 8½ in); 28 pp + fold-out plate

Pictorial card wrappers printed in buff, green and black, tied with orange cord

One full-colour double-page illustration and 11 full-page halftone illustrations

Illustrated: *The Gentle Art of Advertising*, pp 58–69

The Press Art School

131. A half-page drawing in line advertising correspondence courses in art

Published in an insert to the Press Art School brochure, 1919

Procter Bros (Wireworks) Ltd

132. 'The Toasted Cheese Method – This Isn't the Only Way to Catch Mice, Try the Little Nipper'

Full-colour design for show-card and postcard, n.d.

Note: Reproduced as a greetings card by Athena International, London, *c*.1976

133. 'It has been suggested that obsolete tanks should be used as Mouse Traps, but you will find the Little Nipper much more effective'

Full-colour design for press advertisement, n.d. [1919]

Keith Prowse & Co. Ltd

134. 'New machine for automatically securing to you the very seat you require'

A small line illustration

Published: *The Evening News*, 27 Jul 1923

Prudential Assurance Co. Ltd

135. 'A simple device for showing at a glance the position of your insurance – with gramophone adjustment for use at the New Year'

Quarter-page press advertisement in line

Published: *The Evening Standard*, 1 Jan 1934, p.17

Ransomes, Sims & Jefferies

136. 'W. Heath Robinson's Impressions of Ransomes' Motor Mowers', drawings in pen and wash for press advertisements

Published: *The Tatler*, 4 Apr 1928, vol.CVIII, no.1397, full page; *The Sketch*, 3 Apr 1929, p.3, two vignettes used for a half-page advt

Note: Proofs of Heath Robinson designs for advertisements for Ransomes lawnmowers dated 1928 have been seen, some in colour, and with captions in English, Dutch and German.

Société Anonyme des Usines Remy

137. 'Fabrication du Macaroni Remy'

Poster in line for Remy Macaroni, also used as a press advertisement

Published: Wygmael (Brabant), Belgium, 1922

Note: Heath Robinson had also designed a poster advertising Remy's Starch some years earlier.

Rhodian Cigarettes

138. 'The Manufacture of Rhodian Cigarettes'
Quarter-page press advertisement in line
Published: *The Evening Standard*, 1 Jan 1937, p.23

139. 'Testing the Aroma of Rhodian Cigarettes with the New Natural Flavour'
Quarter-page press advertisement in line
Published: *The Evening Standard*, 2 Jan 1939, p.17

Rogers Peet Company

140. *Some Trade Secrets Revealed*, by Rogers Peet Company, New York, n.d. (1927)
248 × 164 mm (9¾ × 6½ in)
A paper folder containing six plates
Six full-page drawings in line. A vignette extracted from one of the drawings is reproduced on the front cover in orange
Illustrated: *Printed Salesmanship*, Cambridge, Massachusetts, Jun 1927, pp 346–7
Reproduced: *The Gentle Art of Advertising*, pp 26–31

Rownson, Drew & Clydesdale, Ltd

141. 'Different methods of overcoming bathroom difficulties'
Full-page, halftone press advertisement
Published: *Town and Country Homes*, Feb 1929, p.71

The Ruberoid Co. Ltd

142. 'Pluvex Roofing Felt', n.d.
A folded sheet with eight small line drawings

Ruston-Bucyrus Ltd

143. *The Gentle Art of Excavating*, W. Heath Robinson, issued with the compliments of Ruston-Bucyrus Ltd, Lincoln, n.d. (*c.*1938)
272 × 222 mm (10¾ × 8¾ in); 12 pp
Light brown card wrappers printed in dark brown
Six full-page halftone illustrations and ten smaller line drawings
Illustrated: *The Gentle Art of Advertising*, pp 11–19; Chris Beetles Ltd exhibition catalogue, 1987, p.127 (2)

Shuck, Maclean & Co. Ltd

144. *Life Without Printing Ink*, Shuck, Maclean & Co. Ltd, n.d.
295 × 237 mm (11⅝ × 9⅜ in)
Wrappers secured by silk bow at top corner
Six full-colour plates, of which one is by WHR
Illustrated: The WHR plate reproduced in monochrome in *Commercial Art*, Jun 1927, vol.II, p.258
Note: Other artists are H.M. Bateman, Alfred Leete, G.E. Studdy, Chas. Graves and D'Egville

145. *Testimonials and Otherwise*, Shuck, Maclean & Co Ltd, n.d.
295 × 237 mm (11⅝ × 9⅜ in)
Wrappers secured by silk bow at top corner
Six full-colour plates, of which one is by WHR
Note: Other artists are John Hassall, Alfred Leete, G.E. Studdy, Fred Buchanan and A.A. Nash

146. *Printing Ink in the Home*, Shuck, Maclean & Co Ltd, n.d. [1930]
295 × 237 mm (11⅝ × 9⅜ in)
Wrappers secured by silk bow at top corner
Six full-colour plates, of which one is by WHR
Note: Other artists are H.M. Bateman, Alfred Leete, G.E. Studdy, Fred Buchanan and D'Egville

The Skefko Ball Bearing Company, Ltd

147. 'Behind the Scenes in a Modern Ball Bearing Factory'
A grey card folder with two halftone plates mounted on the inside
With the compliments of SKF, Christmas 1926
305 × 222 mm (12 × 8¾ in); 4 pp

A. & W. Smith & Co. Ltd

148. 'Seven Stages in the Refining of Sugar'
A halftone show card printed in sepia for A. & W. Smith & Co. Ltd., Eglinton Engine Works, Glasgow, C.5., n.d.
360 × 292 mm (14⅛ × 11½ in)

Smith's Sectric Clocks

149. 'A Good Resolution for the New Year – Install in Every Room Smith's Synchronous Electric Clocks'
Press advertisement in line
Published: *The Evening Standard*, 1 Jan 1934, p.17

150. 'The Sealing-wax Test of the Correct Synchronisation of Smith's Electric Clocks at Noon'
Press advertisement in line
Published: *The Evening Standard*, 1 Jan 1937, p.23

151. 'The Sun Test for Sectric Clocks'
Press advertisement in line
Published: *The Evening Standard*, 2 Jan 1939, p.17

152. 'Plug in at Greenwich – Smith's Sectric Clocks Enable You to Start All the Days of the New Year on Time'
Press advertisement in line
Published: *The Evening Standard*, 1 Jan 1940, p.12
Illustrated: *The Gentle Art of Advertising*, p.71

Spratt's

153. 'The making of Spratt's Bonios'
A line drawing for press advertisement
Published: *Tail Waggers* magazine, *c.*1925

Standard Fireworks

154. 'How Standard Fireworks Are Made' and 'Some Uses for Standard Fireworks'
Two drawings for press advertisements and/or posters, n.d.
Exhibited: Hornsey Library, 13 Jan 1973

Douglas Stuart

155. 'When You're Putting Your Shirt on a Horse. Tell "Duggie" all about it'
Press advertisement in line for Douglas Stuart, bookmaker, Stuart House, Shaftesbury Avenue, London
Published: *Illustrated Sporting and Dramatic News*, 31 Jan 1936 and 2 Apr 1937, back covers

156. 'There's Absolutely No Limit to What You Can Put On a Horse If You – Tell "Duggie" all about it'
Press advertisement in line for Douglas Stuart, bookmaker, Stuart House, Shaftesbury Avenue, London
Published: *Illustrated Sporting and Dramatic News*, 7 Feb 1936 and 28 Feb 1936, back covers

157. 'When Getting a Tip Straight from the Horse's Mouth – Tell "Duggie" all about it'
Press advertisement in line for Douglas Stuart, bookmaker, Stuart House, Shaftesbury Avenue, London
Published: *Illustrated Sporting and Dramatic News*, 14 Feb 1936, back cover

158. 'When Backing a Horse in Your Own Home – Tell "Duggie" all about it'

Press advertisement in line for Douglas Stuart, bookmaker, Stuart House, Shaftesbury Avenue, London

Published: *Illustrated Sporting and Dramatic News*, 21 Feb 1936, 4 Sep 1936 and 5 Feb 37, back covers

159. 'If You're Picking a Horse Blindly – Back It With Your Eyes Open'

Press advertisement in line for Douglas Stuart, bookmaker, Stuart House, Shaftesbury Avenue, London

Published: *Illustrated Sporting and Dramatic News*, 6 Mar 1936, back cover

160. 'If You Must Have Something On, Tell "Duggie" all about it'

Press advertisement in line for Douglas Stuart, bookmaker, Stuart House, Shaftesbury Avenue, London

Published: *Illustrated Sporting and Dramatic News*, 10 Apr 1936, back cover
Illustrated London News, 27 Jun 1936, back cover

161. 'If You Want to be in on a Good Double Event, Tell "Duggie" all about it'

Press advertisement in line for Douglas Stuart, bookmaker, Stuart House, Shaftesbury Avenue, London

Published: *Illustrated Sporting and Dramatic News*, 1 May 1936, back cover

162. 'If You Are About to Put a "Monkey" on a Horse . . . Tell "Duggie" all about it'

Press advertisement in line for Douglas Stuart, bookmaker, Stuart House, Shaftesbury Avenue, London

Published: *Illustrated Sporting and Dramatic News*, 26 Feb 1937, back cover

Thomas Tapling & Co. Ltd

163. 'The Gentle Art of Making Feather Beds' and 'The Gentle Art of Making Down Quilts'

186 × 216 mm (32⅛ × 8½ in)

Two drawings for press advertisements/showcards, n.d.

Illustrated: The latter illustrated in *The Gentle Art of Advertising*, p.87

Thomas & Green Ltd

164. 'The Art of Paper Making as Explained by W. Heath Robinson', a calendar for 1922. Thomas & Green Ltd, Wooburn Green, Bucks 1921

A single board covered in handmade paper

530 × 390 mm (20⅞ × 15⅜ in)

Nine small drawings in full colour plus mounted tear-off date tablet

Produced by G. Heath Robinson & J. Birch Ltd, 17 & 18 Took's Court, London EC4

Also: published as a press advertisement in *The British Printer*, Jan–Feb 1922, vol.34, facing p.228

165. A line drawing of the Thomas & Green works as seen by Heath Robinson. Intended for press advertisements, *c.* Nov 1922

Turnbulls Ltd

166. Five drawings in pen and wash:
a. 'Method of Dyeing Children's Clothes in the Stone Ages'
b. 'Cleaning through the Ages'
c. 'Impressions of the Dyeing Industry'
d. 'Up-to-date Methods in a Modern Dye Works'
e. 'Dyeing in the Past, Present and Future'

Published: As double-page spreads in *Turnbulls Quarterly*, 1929–31

Also available to customers, on application, as prints suitable for framing

Vickery's Ltd

167. 'Interesting Experiments in the Research Department of Vickerys Ltd, Paper Mill Specialities', 'Tripling the Treatment – the Triple Treatment Research Department in Full Swing' and 'Stages in the Evolution of Vickery Doctoring'

Line drawings for press advertisements and wall cards for Vickery Ltd, Lambeth Palace Road, London SE1

Published: As wall-cards on samples of Vickery's paper, n.d.

Illustrated: *The Gentle Art of Advertising*, pp 84–5 (2)

Wagon Repair Company

168. *At Your Service*, a list of agents of the Wagon Repair Company

180 × 120 mm (7⅛ × 4¾ in); 103 pp

Blue cloth blocked in black

Illustrated endpapers in red and black, the front by WHR, the back by Will Owen

C.C. Wakefield & Co. Ltd

169. 'Some of the severe laboratory tests to which Wakefield Castrol Oil is submitted'

A small line illustration

Published: *The Evening News*, 27 Jul 1923

Johnnie Walker

170. Stages in the Manufacture of Johnnie Walker Whisky

Six full-page halftone illustrations, possibly for a calendar, n.d. [1915]

Illustrated: *The Gentle Art of Advertising*, pp 20–25

Reprinted: *The Johnnie Walker Heath Robinson Prints*, 1987, six full-scale reproductions printed in sepia on cream paper, bound calendar style

Watney, Combe, Reid & Co.

171. 'Safety First – The new safety helmet for preventing miners being overcome by thirst in salt mines'

A full-page line drawing printed in blue

Published: *Hand in Hand*, Mar 1921

172. 'Reid's Stout, every sample tested for its strengthening properties before leaving the brewery'

A small line illustration

Published: *The Evening News*, 27 Jul 1923

Webb's Radio

173 'Webb's Radio Carry On and Deliver the Goods', a halftone print in green and black

220 × 560 mm (8⅝ × 22 in)

Note: This design was used to decorate the 'wooden windows' that temporarily replaced the glass windows lost in the Blitz at the shop at 14 Soho St, W1. The design was painted on the substitute windows by Norman Keene.

Wellington & Ward Ltd

174. *The Light Side of Photography* illustrated by W. Heath Robinson, Wellington and Ward Ltd, Elstree, Hertfordshire n.d. (1925)

250 × 185 mm (9⅞ × 7¼ in); 16 pp

Pictorial wrappers

12 full-page halftone illustrations and a cover design in line

Note: These drawings were used for press advertisements in *The New Photographer* in 1925. They were also issued as postcards.

Wright, Layman & Umney Ltd

175. 'Some New Machinery for Putting the Final Touches to Toilet Soap'

Quarter-page press advertisement in line for Wright's Coal Tar Soap

Published: *The Evening Standard*, 1 Jan 1934, p.16

Illustrated: *The Gentle Art of Advertising*, p.70

176. 'Coping with the Extra Demand in Coronation Year. The Wrapping and Packing Department'

Quarter-page press advertisement in line for Wright's Coal Tar Soap

Published: *The Evening Standard*, 1 Jan 1937, p.23

177. 'The Latest Stages in the Development of a Perfect Toilet Soap'

Quarter-page press advertisement in line for Wright's Coal Tar Soap

Published: *The Evening Standard*, 2 Jan 1939, p.17

178. 'Wright's Coal Tar Soap – the Soap for Everybody in the New Year'

Quarter-page press advertisement in line for Wright's Coal Tar Soap

Published: *The Evening Standard*, 1 Jan 1940, p.12

Youngman Ladders

179. 'Take No Chances –' Youngman Ladders, n.d.

166 × 101 mm (6½ × 4 in); 4-page leaflet

Full-page line drawing on the front, printed in brown on pink paper

Zerkall Bütten

180. 'Zerkall Bütten Auf Der Maschine Geschöpft', Papierfabrik Zerkall Renker & Söhne GmbH, Germany, n.d.

Three full-page line drawings printed as postcards on handmade paper

150 × 115 mm (5⅞ × 4½ in)

Note: Reissued in the 1980s, 3 panels, folded zig-zag style, printed in grey on hand-made paper. A set of large hand-coloured proofs of the drawings has also been seen.

PORTRAIT OF THE ARTIST.
Mr. W. Heath Robinson gives a good impression of himself.

284 'Portrait of the Artist: Mr W. Heath Robinson gives a good impression of himself', published in *The London Magazine*, August 1908.

Notes & Acknowledgements

A GENERAL NOTE ON SOURCES

The captions to drawings were often incorporated in the drawing and in most cases are clearly Heath Robinson's own. However, they were sometimes altered by a copywriter, and where this is evident it is noted.

Quotations from letters to Heath Robinson from his agent A.E. Johnson or from companies commissioning work from him are all from letters, currently uncatalogued, in the archive held by the William Heath Robinson Trust.

Introduction

1. *The London Magazine*, vol.20, August 1908, p.624.

2. W. Heath Robinson, *My Line of Life*, Blackie & Son, London, 1938, p.176.

3. *The Studio*, vol.XXI, December 1900, p.209.

4. Grant Richards Archive, University of Illinois Library, Urbana-Champaign, Illinois.

5. Heath Robinson, *My Line of Life*, p.119.

6. Ibid. p.103.

7. *The Advertising World*, December 1915, pp 523-7.

8. *Commercial Art*, vol.II, June 1927, pp 256-9.

Chapter 1

1. 'Canterbury and District Ironmongers' Assistants' Association: Lecture on Asbestos', *The Whitstable Times and Tankerton Press*, 2 July 1932.

Chapter 3

1. Percy V. Bradshaw, *Art in Advertising*, The Press Art School, London, n.d. [1925], p.158.

Chapter 4

1. Heath Robinson, *My Line of Life*, p.174.

2. 'Hamilton', 'Humour in Advertising', *Commercial Art*, vol.II, March 1927, p.115.

Chapter 6

1. *Nottingham, 'The Queen City of the Midlands'*, official guide, sixth edition, 1927, accessed via nottshistory.org.uk.

Chapter 7

1. *The Studio*, vol.CII, July 1931, p.21.

2. William Heath Robinson (illus.) and Anthony Armstrong (text), *The Story of Cocktails*, Canadian Pacific Steamship Company, London, 1932.

3. Heath Robinson, *My Line of Life*, p.179.

Chapter 8

1. Bradshaw, *Art in Advertising*, pp 326-9.

ACKNOWLEDGEMENTS

The listing of Heath Robinson's published drawings for advertising would be less complete than it is, were it not for the earlier efforts of others on which it has been possible to build, and access to private archives and collections. In particular I must express gratitude to the late Quentin Robinson who compiled *The Gentle Art of Advertising* published by Duckworth in 1979; to the late J.-P. Marix Evans, formerly chairman of Lamson Industries (UK) Ltd, for giving up a great deal of time to explain the early history of the Lamson Paragon companies and for granting access to material relating to those companies and to Chas. Ed. Potter; to Anthony Hussey for giving unlimited access to the Connolly Bros archives; to Austin Reeve for making available the results of his earlier researches into Heath Robinson's advertising work; to David M. Firth for information regarding Firth Brothers furniture advertisements; and to Nicolas McDowall for drawing my attention to the drawings for the Cropwell Herd and for providing me with images of them.

Further image credits:

Central Press / Getty Images: frontispiece

Keystone / Getty Iimages: 147

Malcolm Warrington / fotoLibra: 283

Private collections: 6, 79, 80.

William Heath Robinson Trust: 3, 9, 186, 187, 205, 277.

All others are from the author's collection.

INDEX

Page numbers in *italics* refer to illustrations.

THE END

285 'The End', from *Light on Leather*, Connolly Bros (Curriers) Ltd, London, 1922.